rororo Sprachen
Herausgegeben von Ludwig Moos

Drop Them a Line befaßt sich mit Briefen, wie sie jeder im Beruf schreiben, lesen oder beantworten muß, der mit englischsprachigen Geschäftspartnern zu tun hat. Bewerbungen, Angebote, Beschwerden, Einladungen, Memos oder Kostenvoranschläge sind nur einige der vielen Schriftformen, deren Sprache und Stil das Buch einüben hilft. Sie lernen, wie Sie sich einfach, aber effektiv ausdrücken und zu jeder Situation im Geschäftsalltag die passende Wendung finden. Und damit der Stoff nicht zu trocken wird, ist er eingebettet in nicht allzu ernsthafte Geschichten, wie sie das Geschäftsleben schreibt.

Bryan Hemming ist Native Speaker und arbeitet als Sprachlehrer in Firmen, an den Universitäten Heidelberg und Warwick sowie an der Berufsakademie Mannheim.

Mitgearbeitet an dem Buch haben Dr. René Bosewitz und Robert Kleinschroth, von denen das Konzept und die bisher erschienenen Bände der Reihe *Business English* stammen: *Manage in English* (60137), *How to Phone Effectively* (60139), *Better than the Boss* (60138) und *Test Your Management Skills* (60260).

René Bosewitz ist Native Speaker und unterrichtet an der Berufsakademie Mannheim. In einer deutschen Zweigstelle der London Chamber of Commerce bereitet er Firmenangehörige auf einschlägige sprachliche Prüfungen vor. Er trainiert zudem seit vielen Jahren Topmanager aus Banken und Industrie in Business English.

Robert Kleinschroth unterrichtet Englisch am Gymnasium und an der Universität Heidelberg. Er hat zwanzig Jahre Praxis in der Erwachsenenbildung und leitete fünfzehn Jahre lang die Sprachabteilung eines Großunternehmens.

BRYAN HEMMING
UNTER MITARBEIT VON RENÉ BOSEWITZ
UND ROBERT KLEINSCHROTH

DROP THEM A LINE

BUSINESS ENGLISH IM SCHRIFTVERKEHR

Rowohlt
rororo

Originalausgabe
Veröffentlicht im Rowohlt Taschenbuch Verlag GmbH,
Reinbek bei Hamburg, Februar 1997

Umschlaggestaltung Barbara Hanke (Illustration Cathrin Günther)
Layout Anne Drude und Alexander Urban
Satz OCR-A und Stone, PostScript Linotype Library,
QuarkXPress 3.31 (Dolev 800)
Druck und Bindung Clausen & Bosse, Leck
Printed in Germany
1490-ISBN 3 499 60261 X

Inhalt

Vorwort

Drop Them a Line macht Sie vertraut mit den wichtigsten Bereichen des geschäftlichen Briefverkehrs. Die Korrespondenz ist in eine Rahmenhandlung eingebunden und spiegelt die Entwicklung der Firma Onions wider. Onions ist ein Hersteller von Heizgeräten, der sich unbedingt vergrößern will. Sie verfolgen den Aufstieg der Firma und lernen englische Handelskorrespondenz vor dem Hintergrund des Geschäftsablaufs: Eine Anfrage geht ein, ein Angebot wird gemacht, ein Auftrag wird erteilt – wenn alles gut geht. Leider ist das nicht immer der Fall. Da werden Rechnungen nicht bezahlt, Lieferungen verzögern sich, Kunden beschweren sich, um nur einige der täglichen Pannen zu erwähnen, die viel Mühe kosten. Überdies drängt Onions mit Macht auf fremde Märkte. Nach anfänglichen Schwierigkeiten gelingt es sogar, die chinesische Mauer zu überwinden. Auf dem langen Weg der Firma bis zur Gründung einer Niederlassung im Fernen Osten werden Sie, neben manchem kleinen *joke*, die wichtigsten Wendungen des englischen Geschäftsbriefs auflesen und den zugrunde liegenden Geschäftsvorgang verstehen.
Es bietet sich an, die Kapitel in ihrer Reihenfolge zu lesen. Doch ist das Buch zugleich auch ein praktisches Nachschlagewerk. Wie auch immer Sie es nutzen, die klare Struktur erleichtert Ihnen das Lernen und Verstehen.

➢ **Focus:** Zu Beginn eines jeden Kapitels wird eine typische Situation des Geschäftsalltags erläutert: der Auftrag, die Beschwerde, die Bewerbung ...

D **Dialogue:** Die Mitarbeiter der Firma suchen im Gespräch nach einer Lösung des Problems. Aus diesem Gespräch entwickelt sich die Korrespondenz. Dadurch wird die Funktion des Briefes im Geschäftsablauf verständlich.

Drop Them a Line: Der so entstandene Brief kann als Muster für die eigene Korrespondenz dienen. Wie Sie diese Vorlage Ihren Bedürfnissen anpassen können, erfahren Sie im folgenden Teil des Kapitels.

↔ **Put It Another Way:** Zu jedem Briefmuster erhalten Sie einen Vorrat alternativer Redewendungen mit ihren deutschen Bedeutungen.

Vocabulary: Eine englisch-deutsche Wortschatzliste sorgt dafür, daß Sie alles verstehen. Es ist ganz einfach.

Brain Work: Nicht ganz so einfach, aber lernintensiv! (Deshalb haben wir das Symbol auch dunkler gemacht.) Sie sollen den Wortschatz und die typischen Wendungen des Geschäftsbriefs anwenden. Zu den Übungen finden Sie einen Schlüssel im Anhang, aber widerstehen Sie bitte der Versuchung zu schummeln.

Letter Box: Wenn es nicht ohne Grammatik geht, finden Sie hier die Regel und eine Übung. Daneben aber auch Hinweise zu so wichtigen Dingen wie den Möglichkeiten der Anrede oder des Briefschlusses.

Letter Functions: Im Anhang finden Sie ein systematisches Verzeichnis mit den wichtigsten Wendungen des englischen Geschäftsbriefs – den Baukasten für Ihre Briefe.

Viel Spaß beim Korrespondieren.

Problems of Style

CONTENTS

Joke Time

A boss was saying goodbye to her secretary after years of working together. "I'll be sorry to lose[1] you," she said. "You've been exactly[2] like my daughter[3]". "Really?" said the secretary a little surprised[4]. "Yes, you've been rude, lazy and bad-mannered[5] for all the years I've known you".

Ian Burns, the personnel manager[6] at Corbetts, said one morning to a trainee[7]
"Jones, I don't know how we will get along without you[8] but starting on the first of next month we are going to have a really good try".

1 verlieren 2 genau 3 Tochter 4 erstaunt 5 unhöflich, faul und ungezogen 6 Personalleiter 7 Auszubildender 8 ohne Sie zurechtkommen

➢ Focus: Style in the business letter

When speaking English you can be informal but when writing business letters you must remember to be polite, formal but not pompous or old-fashioned. Above all keep the letter simple.

D Dialogues: Terry gets a lesson

Corbetts is a wholesale company in England. They distribute food from the producer to small retailers, usually corner shops.
In the personnel department Mrs Brookes (**B**), the head of sales, is talking to Ian Burns (**I**), the personnel manager, about a new trainee, Terry Jones.

B: Well, I can't believe the letter that Jones wanted to send to one of our suppliers. Luckily I saw it first and stopped him sending it.
I: Why what's wrong now? I've had nothing but complaints about young Terry.
B: Here's the letter. See for yourself.
I: Let me just read that, let's see (*Ian reads the letter*)
"Dear Bob", good start, okay,
"Thanks a lot for the offer of chocolate biscuits type 'Nutty Crunch' – especially as I like them myself. Your conditions are 20 quid for a box of fifty packets if we buy more than ten boxes. That's good because we need 12 boxes. Can you let us have them by next Wednesday? We really need them.
And another thing, the tins of baked beans you sent us last month ... they were no good. The customers complained, something about too much tomato sauce and not enough beans. Sorry, but if you can't send us better quality goods we must find somebody else to get us the beans.
Yours faithfully
Terry Jones"

Good Grief! I think I'd better have a few words with him straight away.

B: Well be careful about the words you use. Remember his dad is on the board of directors and his family is in all kinds of business a-round here.

Let's see what Ian Burns says to Terry (T).

I: Now about this letter to a supplier. Have you never written a letter before?

T: Actually yes. My girlfriend lives in Scotland and we can't afford to see eachother every weekend so I write lots of letters.

I: Well, I can believe that but I'm talking about business letters. Formal commercial correspondence.

T: What was wrong with it? The spelling, the grammar?

I: No, it was the way the letter was written.

T: You mean I shouldn't have written it on the typewriter?

I: I mean the style. It was too informal, you were too friendly and too direct.

T: Well, Mr Miller in sales says you should be friendly when talking to clients.

I: That's on the phone when you already know the client. Right, let me try to help. Look here, I'll write some parts of your letter down on the left and I'll write what you should put on the right.

↔ Put it Another Way: Formal and informal

Here is what Ian Burns wrote.

Informal letter style	Formal letter style	German
thanks a lot for	*thank you very much for*	vielen Dank für
if we buy more than	*if we purchase in excess of*	wenn wir mehr als ... kaufen
can you let us have them?	*would it be possible to receive the goods?*	wäre es möglich, daß wir die Waren erhalten?
and another thing	*in addition to this*	darüber hinaus

were no good	*were of inferior quality*	waren von minderer Qualität
sorry, but if you	*we regret to say that if it*	wir würden es bedauern, wenn
can't send us	*is impossible to supply us with*	aber sollte es Ihnen nicht möglich sein, uns ... zu liefern
we must find	*we will be forced to find*	wir werden gezwungen sein, zu finden
somebody else	*an alternative supplier*	ein anderer Lieferant
to get us beans	*provide us with these goods*	uns mit diesen Waren zu beliefern

(D) Back to Terry Jones and Ian Burns

I: There you are, Terry. And by the way what is the supplier's second name?
T: It's Jones.
I: Well, don't you think you should call him Mr Jones since he is a supplier.
T: Maybe, but I think I should call him Bob since he is my uncle!

(V) Vocabulary: To help you understand

biscuit	Keks
board of directors	Vorstand
complaint	Beschwerde
condition	Bedingung
corner shop	Laden an der Ecke
dad	Papa
department	Abteilung
distribute	verteilen

especially	besonders
food	Lebensmittel
good grief!	mein Gott!
head of sales	Leiter der Verkaufsabteilung
I'd better	ich sollte/es wäre besser
luckily	zum Glück
old-fashioned	altmodisch
polite	höflich
pompous	schwülstig
quid (slang for pound)	Eier (umgangssprachlich für Geld)
retailer	Einzelhändler
spelling	Rechtschreibung
supplier	Lieferant
tin of baked beans	Dose mit gebackenen Bohnen
trainee	Auszubildende/r
wholesale	Großhandel

B Brain Work One: Let's practise style

Here is another letter from Terry. Now it is your turn to put the style right. Below you can see some phrases. Try and put them into the letter to make it more formal.

to provide us with the goods
were of inferior quality
an alternative supplier
we will be forced to find
thank you very much for
if we purchase in excess of
in addition to this

Dear Miss Weakley

1) *Thanks a lot for* the offer of frozen vegetables. The price is £7.50 for a five kilo bag 2) *if we buy more than* 50 bags. 3) *And another thing* we must say is that the first class English beef burgers 4) *were no good*. We regret to say that if it is impossible supply us with better quality products 5) *we must find* 6) *somebody* 7) *to get us the beef burgers.*

Yours faithfully

Letter Box: Starting and ending a letter

You can start a letter with Dear Sir, Dear Sirs, Dear Madam, Dear Mrs Jackson, Dear Snuggy Pops, Dear Sue, My Dearest Darling, To the World's Greatest Lover etc. Please do not forget it is important to follow the rule below. Also note that we do not normally address the bank manager 'Snuggy Pops'. Of course this depends on your bank manager and you. Remember!

Dear Sir	starts a letter to a man whose name you do not know.
Dear Madam	starts a letter to a woman whose name you do not know
Dear Sirs	starts a letter to a company.
Dear Sir or Madam	starts a letter where you do not know the name or sex.

And the letter ends with *Yours faithfully.*

When you know the name of the person you are writing to start with:

Dear Mr Beavis
Dear Dr Johnson
Dear Mrs Whitehouse

And the letter ends with *Yours sincerely.*

Do not start a letter and use both first and second name:
Dear Mr Patrick Beavis or Dear Dr Susan Whitehouse

If you start a letter:
Dear Lover Boy or Dearest Snuffle Wuffle

You can write what you want at the end!

PS If you do write to your bank manager and start Dearest Snuffle Wuffle etc. you can write whatever you like but 'Yours faithfully' is probably too formal.

B Brain Work Two: Quiz time

1) If a letter starts with Dear Mr Clinton it ends with ...?
2) If a letter ends with Yours faithfully it starts with ...?
3) If a letter starts with Dear Sir or Madam it ends with ...?
4) If you write a letter to somebody and you do not know their name or sex you start with ...?
5) If you write to Andreas Stecker, you start with ... and you end with ...? In this case be formal.

Enquiries

CONTENTS

Joke Time

The boss was interviewing[1] a young woman for the post[2] of secretary.
"How many words can you type a minute Miss Stevens?" he asked.
"Long words or short words?" she queried.[3]

A rather timid[4] office clerk came into Bob Onion's office.
"Excuse me, Mr Onion, I'm really sorry to bother [5] you right now, but you see I've been here five years now and my wife said it's time I was given a raise[6]. What do you think, Mr Onion?"
Bob Onion thought about this for a moment and then replied[7] "Well, I think it's fine by me but let me just check with my wife if you don't mind[8]".

1 Vorstellungsgespräch führen mit 2 Stelle 3 fragen 4 schüchtern 5 stören 6 Lohnerhöhung 7 antworten 8 nichts dagegen haben

Focus: Enquiries – an important first step

This type of letter is used to find customers, suppliers, agents and distributors. Most enquiries are short if the enquiry comes from buyers who want to place a limited order. However, if they want special conditions for regular orders or the right to sell for a producer the enquirers must try to sell the proposal.

The basic enquiry contains:

1) How you got the name of the potential supplier
2) The condition of the local market for the goods in question
3) What you want from the supplier, for example, catalogues, samples, price lists.

Dialogue: Introducing Onions

Onions is a British heating engineering company which produces boilers and other equipment. They are a small but growing company always interested in expanding. We will get to know some of the managers and other staff in their offices near Birmingham. Here we meet Ian Miller (**IM:**) and Gerry Murry (**GM:**) in the purchasing department.

IM: We need to reduce the costs of our units if we want to stay competitive.

GM: That's why I'm looking for other suppliers. Last month I was at a couple of trade fairs, one in Rome and another in Thailand.

IM: You certainly get about, Gerry. Did you get any contacts?

GM: Contacts, well, actually yes and no.

IM: I see, well, I was at a small trade fair near Bradford and I ´ve seen one or two things in the press.

GM: Ha, Bradford, I haven't been there in years.

IM: No, you don't have time, I mean with all the work and travel.

GM: Yes, I know. Life can be very hard, it's true.

Drop Them a Line: Enquiries to companies in Russia and Italy

Ian Miller and Gerry Murry write two letters:

Dear Sirs

We have seen your advertisement in 'The Engineer' and would appreciate it if you would kindly let us have details concerning your water pumps.
Please send us a quotation for the items listed on the form enclosed. Give your prices c.i.f. Hull. We would also like to know delivery times and terms of payment. In addition can you also indicate the types of discount you offer for regular and bulk orders.
If your prices are competitive and your products come up to our expectations we will be pleased to place substantial and regular orders.
We are looking forward to hearing from you soon

Yours faithfully
Ian Miller

Dear Sirs

We saw your pumps and other equipment demonstrated at the Mech-Tech engineering trade fair in Rome last month and would be grateful if you could send us information about your water pumps.
Will you kindly quote prices c.i.f. Hull for the units on the enclosed list. As well as this please inform us as to delivery times, terms of payment and sorts of dicounts offered for regular and large orders.
If your prices are favourable and your products meet with our approval we will be happy to place large orders on a regular basis.
We would appreciate a prompt answer

Yours faithfully
Gerry Murry

Both letters ask for the same information but have different phrases to say the same thing. It is important to be able to say the same thing in different ways to avoid writing boring letters with limited flexibility of style.

(V) Vocabulary: To help you understand

actually	eigentlich
advertisement	Annonce, Anzeige
agent	Vertreter
appreciate	zu schätzen wissen
basic	einfach
boring	langweilig
bulk order	Großauftrag
buyer	Käufer, Einkäufer
catalogue	Katalog
CIF (Cost, Insurance, Freight)	Kosten, Versicherung, Fracht
come up to	entsprechen
competitive	konkurrenzfähig
concerning	bezüglich
contain	enthalten
customer	Kunde
delivery times	Lieferzeiten
discount	Rabatt
distributor	Verteiler
enclosed	beiliegend
enquirer	Fragesteller/in
enquiry	Anfrage
equipment	Geräte, Ausrüstung
expectations	Erwartungen
form	Formular
heating engineering	Heizungsinstallateur
however	jedoch
in the press	in der Presse
indicate	deuten auf
item	Artikel
kindly	freundlicherweise
let us have	schicken Sie uns
limited	beschränkt

list	auflisten
local market	örtlicher Markt
look forward to	sich freuen auf
offer	Angebot
payment	Zahlung
place an order	einen Auftrag erteilen
post	Stelle
price list	Preisliste
proposal	Vorschlag
purchasing department	Einkaufsabteilung
quotation	Kostenvoranschlag
regular	regelmäßig
regular order	regelmäßiger Auftrag
right	Recht
sample	Muster
stay competitive	konkurrenzfähig bleiben
substantial	wesentlich
supplier	Lieferant
term	Bedingung
trade fair	Messe
unit	Einheit
water pumps	Wasserpumpen
you certainly get about	Du kommst wirklich viel herum

↔ Put It Another Way: Alternative phrases

Here are some phrases together with alternatives. Take a good look and check the meaning with the German.

would appreciate it	*would be grateful*	wären dankbar
kindly let us have	*please send us*	bitte schicken Sie uns
details concerning	*information about*	Informationen über
we would like to know	*inform us as to*	bitte teilen Sie uns mit
as well	*in addition*	auch
if your prices are favourable	*if your prices are competitive*	wenn Ihre Preise konkurrenzfähig sind

come up to our expectations	*meet with our approval*	unseren Erwartungen entsprechen
substantial	*large*	wesentlich
we are looking foward to hearing from you soon	*we would appreciate a prompt answer**	wir freuen uns auf eine baldige Antwort

* "we would appreciate a prompt answer" sounds a little more formal than "we are looking forward to hearing from you"

B Brain Work Three: What's the English for ...?

Here is your chance to do some work. Have a try at finding the English for the following sentences. The answers are in this chapter. Good luck!

1) Bitte teilen Sie uns mit
2) Wenn Ihre Preise konkurrenzfähig sind
3) Wenn Ihre Waren unseren Erwartungen entsprechen
4) Wir haben Ihre Anzeige in ... gesehen
5) Bitte machen Sie uns ein Angebot über

B Brain Work Four: Complete the letter

Please complete the following enquiry. The words you need are below. Use each word only once.

1) approval	2) in addition	3) competitive	4) grateful
5) concerning	6) terms	7) quotation	8) substantial
9) enclosed			

Dear Sirs

We saw your advertisement in last week's 'Gardening Now' and would be ... (a) ... if you would let us have information ... (b) ... your garden tools. Please send us a ... (c) ... for the items on the ... (d) ... list ... (e) ... we would also like to know delivery times, ... (f) ... of payment and the types of discount offered for ... (g) ... and regular orders.
If your prices are ... (h) ... and the quality of your tools meets our ... (i) ... we will place a large order.

Yours faithfully

Letter Box: Using "would" and "could"

To make your letters more polite you should use verbs like *would* and *could.* In fact this makes letters sound both polite and more formal.

Send us details about your products clearly sounds rude
Please send us ... is acceptable and polite enough but
Would you please send us ... is the usual form of request.

We want to have the goods next week would be OK to somebody you know but certainly not OK to a person you have never met. It sounds too direct.

We would like to have the goods next week is fine.
Could you please send us the goods next week? is more polite.

If you wish to sound even more polite and perhaps speculative:
Would it be possible for you to send the goods next week?

We were wondering if it might be possible for you to ...? This is asking for a favour and is very polite.

B Brain Work Five: Be polite!

Please make the following sentences polite. Use the examples in the Letter Box to help you.

Example: Give us information about your product.
Answer: Would/Could you please give us information about your product?

1) We want brochures about your tools.
2) Let us have your terms this week.
3) Tell us what types of discounts you offer.
4) Send us details about your wines and spirits.
5) Quote your prices c.i.f. Melbourne.
6) We want delivery dates and discount details.

Offers

CONTENTS

Joke Time

We were introduced[1] to Onions in the last chapter. The boss of Onions, Bob Onion, wanted to promote[2] one of his junior managers to the senior executive[3] level. He handed out a questionnaire[4] to the possible candidates.
One of the questions was: Do you believe that you have executive potential?
One of the candidates wrote in answer: I think I have executive potential because I like to be alone, I never get lonely[5] and I would like to work in a private office on my own and I don't care[6] if people say bad things about me.

One day Wendy Dawson, Gerry Murry's secretary, went into his office and said: Please, Mr Murry, can I have two weeks off work?[7]
Gerry Murry: What for?
Wendy Dawson: Well, you see I'm getting married[8].
Gerry Murry: You've only just come back from you summer holiday!
Why didn't you get married then?
Wendy Dawson: What? And ruin my holiday?

1 vorgestellt 2 befördern 3 Geschäftsleitung 4 Fragebogen 5 einsam 6 es ist mir egal
7 zwei Wochen frei 8 heiraten

Focus: Offers – answering an enquiry

After the enquiry has been received the potential supplier will send the information (this could include catalogues, brochures, samples, details about prices, payment, delivery dates and discounts) requested.
The offer tells the customer that the seller is prepared to sell certain goods for a specific price and on certain conditions or terms.
There are unsolicited offers (a seller writes to a customer without an enquiry) and solicited offers (a seller writes in response to an enquiry).
The person submitting the offer may include all or some of the following:

1) There will be a time limit – there must be an acceptance in two, three weeks
2) The offer may be without engagement – not legally binding
3) Prices may be subject to change without notice
4) Prices, delivery dates, terms of payment and delivery, quantity, type and quality of goods as well as details about any discounts.

Dialogue – Discussing offers

At the engineering company, Onions, Gerry Murry (**GM**) and Ian Miller (**IM**) are looking at the offers they received in reply to their letters.

IM: Take a look at these offers, Gerry. I think the offer from Russia is best.
GM: Really? Where is their factory? Moscow? Petersberg? Somebody might need to go out there and check things out. I've never been there, romantic places with cheap drink and food, I'll bet, vodka, champagne, caviar.
IM: Hmm, interesting you say that. I don't know if it's cheap but they probably have drink and food in Pomsk.
GM: Pomsk?! Where's that?
IM: Siberia, Central Siberia, not too far from Mongolia actually.
GM: Well, let's look at the offer from Rome and then the Russian one.

Drop Them a Line: Receiving two offers

Ian Miller received a letter and Gerry Murry received a letter. Now have a look at both. Note the style and words used.

Dear Mr Miller

Many thanks for you enquiry dated 20th November. We appreciate your interest in our water pumps.
As requested we are sending you enclosed information about our products as well as delivery times, terms of payment and discounts.
By the same post we are also sending you samples of our water pumps.
The quantity discounts given in our price list vary depending on the size of the order. A cash discount is also allowed for payment within two months. Our prices are quoted c.i.f. Hull.
Delivery can be effected on receipt of your order. This offer is valid for two weeks.
We are looking forward to hearing from you, and assure you that your order will receive immediate attention.

Yours sincerely
A. Popov

Dear Mr Murry

We are glad to learn from your letter of 20th November that you are interested in our pumps and we are pleased to send you a current price list together with our terms of business and details of our trade discounts.
We are sending you samples of our pumps by airmail.
If we receive your order before 1st. January we will grant you an early order discount of 10%
This offer must be withdrawn after 14 days as demand for our products is high.
Please let us know your requirements soon

Yours faithfully
V. Antonini

(V) Vocabulary: To help you understand

acceptance	Annahme
allow	gewähren
appreciate	gerne zur Kenntnis nehmen
assure	versichern
attention; your order will receive ~	Ihre Bestellung wird bearbeitet
bet	wetten
brochure	Prospekt
by the same post	mit gleicher Post
cash discount	Skonto
catalogue	Katalog
certain	bestimmt
cheap	billig
conditions	Bedingungen
current	aktuell
delivery	Lieferung
delivery date	Liefertermin
depending on	abhängig von
discount	Rabatt
early order discount	Frühdispositionsrabatt
effect	ausführen
enquiry	Anfrage
factory	Fabrik
goods	Waren
immediate	sofortig
include	einschließen
legally binding	verbindlich
offer	Angebot
on receipt	nach Eingang
prepared	bereit
probably	wahrscheinlich
quantity discount	Mengenrabatt

receive	erhalten
reply	Antwort
request	bitten, Bitte
requirement	Bedarf
response; in ~ to you enquiry	in Beantwortung Ihrer Anfrage
sample	Muster
seller	Verkäufer
size	Größe
solicit	verlangen
subject to change without notice	Preisänderung vorbehalten
submit	einreichen, unterbreiten
supplier	Lieferant
term	Bedingung
terms of payment	Zahlungsbedingungen
trade discount	Händlerrabatt
unsolicited	unverlangt, nicht bestellt
valid	gültig
withdraw an offer	ein Angebot zurückziehen
without engagement	ohne Verpflichtung

↔ Put It Another Way: Alternative phrases

To start a letter

we were glad/pleased to receive your enquiry dated ...	wir haben uns über Ihre Anfrage vom ... gefreut
we refer to your enquiry of ...	wir beziehen uns auf Ihre Anfrage vom ...
we appreciate your interest in ...	wir freuen uns über Ihr Interesse an ...
as requested we are sending you ...	wunschgemäß, schicken wir Ihnen ...

Some terms and prices

our prices are quoted ...	unsere Preise verstehen sich ...
our prices include packing and carriage	unsere Preise schließen Verpackung und Transport ein

transport and other charges to be borne by the purchaser	Transportkosten und andere Kosten zu Lasten des Käufers
we grant a discount of ... %	wir gewähren einen Rabatt von ... %

Some conditions

this offer is without engagement	dieses Angebot ist unverbindlich
this offer is firm/valid for ...	dieses Angebot ist ... gültig/fest für
all prices are subject to ...	alle Preise unterliegen ...
while stocks last	solange der Vorrat reicht

Ending a letter

we assure you that your order will be performed to your entire satisfaction	wir versichern Ihnen, daß Ihr Auftrag zu Ihrer vollen Zufriedenheit ausgeführt wird
you can rely on the careful execution of your order	Sie können sich auf die sorgfältige Ausführung Ihres Auftrages verlassen
we look forward to doing business with you	wir freuen uns darauf, mit Ihnen ins Geschäft zu kommen

B Brain Work Six: Sort out the letter

You have had a hard day. You wrote a letter but it is mixed up. The sentences are in the wrong order. Please sort out the problem.

a) Yours sincerely
b) Dear Mr Wilson
c) We look forward to the pleasure of doing business with you.
d) We were pleased to receive your enquiry dated ...
e) As requested we are sending you a catalogue and price list.
f) Please note that this offer and discount is valid for two weeks.
g) We are also pleased to grant you a discount of 10% for an early order.

B Brain Work Seven: What's the English for ...?

And now more Brain Work. Over to you!
Use the glossary and vocabulary from the chapter to match the German to the English.

1) Solange der Vorrat reicht	a) Our prices are quoted net
2) Wir danken Ihnen für Ihre Anfrage	b) We are willing to grant a special trade discount
3) Wir fügen unsere Preisliste bei	c) Please note that
4) Unsere Preise verstehen sich netto	d) We enclose our price-list
5) Wir sind bereit, einen Sonderhändlerrabatt zu gewähren	e) While stocks last
6) Nehmen Sie bitte zur Kenntnis, daß	f) We thank you for your offer

Letter Box: Short and long forms

In business and official letters you should not use short forms. For example:

We've received your offer	should be	*We have ...*
We're interested in your carpets		*We are ...*
I'm the manager of sales		*I am ...*
John'll write the letter		*John will ...*

Or:

She'd like to have a catalogue	*She would ...*
She'd quoted the price c.i.f.	*She had ...*
He's outside	*He is ...*
He's sent the fax	*He has ...*

The same with negatives:

We won't order the goods	*We will not ...*
We haven't sent the price-list	*We have not ...*
It isn't valid	*It is not ...*
He didn't receive the letter	*He did not ...*

B Brain Work Eight: Replace the short forms

This chapter was hard? Well, when you have done this little job have a rest! Use the Letter Box above to help you change the short forms and make the sentences formal.

1) We're sending you information as requested.
2) Your order'll receive immediate attention.
3) We'd like a special discount.
4) He didn't send the letter on Tuesday.
5) It's very expensive.
6) The firm hasn't granted a discount.

Orders

CONTENTS

Joke Time

At Onions a clerk[1] goes in to see Bob Onion.
Clerk: Excuse me, Mr Onion but I've been here now fifteen years and that means fifteen years of experience[2]. I think it's time I had a rise[3].
Onion: That's not fifteen years of experience. You see, you've had one year of experience fifteen times.

1 Büroangestellte/r 2 Erfahrung 3 Gehaltserhöhung

Focus: Orders – accepting an offer

If the offer from the seller is acceptable to the buyer he or she will place an order. Sometimes a firm will send a special order form, at other times orders are placed over the phone. However, an order should be confirmed in writing if it is placed over the phone. If an order form is sent, a covering letter should be enclosed because it makes clear and confirms agreed conditions such as delivery dates and discounts.

Dialogue: Discussing the placement of an order

Gerry Murry (**GM**) and Ian Miller (**IM**) are discussing an order for water pumps with Bob Onion (**BO**).

BO: So what do you think, the Russian pumps, cheaper but more risky or place an order for the Italian pumps?
GM: I think the Italian company would be better, the samples were better quality.
IM: Yes, but the Russian pumps were good enough for what we need. What's more they are 30% cheaper for large orders. We could place other orders for pipes and cables with Popov's if this order is okay.
BO: Good thinking, Ian. That's what I like to see, enterprising positive thinking! Let's place an order with these Russians.
IM: Right, I'll write a letter straight away.

Drop Them a Line: An order to the Russians

So, after the meeting Ian writes to Popov's:

Dear Mr. Popov

Thank you for your quotation and terms of ... as well as the sample pump.
We have tested your product and are pleased to place the following order for 400 water pumps type T82B.
For your information we have instructed our bank here in Birmingham to open an irrevocable letter of credit in your favour payable at the International Trade Bank in Pomsk.

The sales conditions are as follows:

Price:	£25.50 per pump
Packing:	cases lined with styrofoam
Payment:	irrevocable letter of credit
Delivery:	by 1st May at the latest in Liverpool

We must point out that the quality must correspond to the sample supplied. If this order is completed to our satisfaction we will place regular orders with your firm.

Yours sincerely

Ian Miller
Chief Buyer

(V) Vocabulary: To help you understand

accept	annehmen
agreed condition	vereinbarte Bedingung
as well as	sowie
at the latest	spätestens
buyer	Käufer
case	Kiste
clerk	Büroangestellte
complete	ausführen
condition	Bedingung
confirm	bestätigen
correspond	entsprechen
covering letter	Begleitbrief
delivery date	Liefertermin
discount	Rabatt
enclose	beilegen
enterprising	unternehmungslustig
experience	Erfahrung
following	folgende
for your information	zu Ihrer Information
however	jedoch

in writing	schriftlich
in your favour	zu Ihren Gunsten
instruct	anweisen
irrevocable letter of credit	unwiderrufliches Akkreditiv
lined with styrofoam	mit Schaumstoff ausgekleidet
order	Auftrag
order form	Bestell-Formular
payable	zahlbar
pipe	Rohr
place an order	Auftrag erteilen
pleased to	sich freuen, etwas zu tun
point out	hinweisen auf
quotation	Preisangabe
raise	Gehaltserhöhung
regular/regularly	regelmäßig
risky	riskant
sales condition	Verkaufsbedingung
sample	Muster
term	Bedingung
to our satisfaction	zu unser Zufriedenheit
what's more	außerdem

↔ Put It Another Way: Alternative phrases

To start

we were pleased to receive...	wir haben uns gefreut ... zu bekommen
many thanks for ...	vielen Dank für ...
please let us have ...	bitte senden Sie uns ...
kindly supply ...	bitte liefern Sie ...

Conditions

please arrange early delivery	bitte sorgen Sie für baldige Lieferung
I look forward to receiving ... within ... days	ich freue mich darauf, ... zu erhalten innerhalb ... Tagen
please advise/notify us	bitte teilen Sie uns mit

as soon as the goods are shipped	sobald die Güter abgesandt worden sind
please despatch the goods by rail	bitte senden Sie die Waren mit der Bahn

Ending the letter

we request/ask that you give this order prompt attention	wir bitten Sie, diesen Auftrag sofort zu erledigen
we shall place further orders with you if this order is satisfactorily executed	wir werden Ihnen weitere Aufträge erteilen, wenn dieser Auftrag zufriedenstellend ausgeführt wird

B Brain Work Nine: Sort out a letter

Time for you to do a bit of work. Please put the following parts of a letter in the correct order.Don't forget to use the alternative phrases in 'Put It Another Way'.

1) .... a) Yours sincerely
2) .... b) We shall place further orders with you if this order is satisfactorily executed
3) .... c) We were pleased to receive your quotation of 12th May
4) .... d) Kindly supply us with five kilos of first quality English Tea
5) .... e) Please arrange an early delivery and notify us as soon as the goods are shipped
6) .... f) Dear Mrs. Jackson

B Brain Work Ten: What's the English for ...?

Here is a nice simple job for you to do. Have fun! Please put the English word with the German word.

1) condition	a) Muster
2) in writing	b) einen Auftrag erteilen
3) place an order	c) Bedingung
4) enclose	d) bestätigen
5) sample	f) schriftlich
6) confirm	g) beilegen

B Brain Work Eleven: Put in the right words

How do you feel? Just a bit more Brain Work.
Please put the following words in the sentences. Use each word once.

payable quotation place point satisfaction irrevocable

1) The letter of credit is ... at your local bank.
2) Thank you for your ... and terms of delivery.
3) I ought to ... out that the quality of the product must be good.
4) We are pleased to ... the following order.
5) We will open an ... letter of credit.
6) If the products are to our ... we will place more orders.

Chapter 5

Acknowledgements

CONTENTS

Focus: Acknowledging an order
Dialogue: The Russians wonder how to acknowledge Onions' order
Drop Them a Line: A correct acknowledgement
Put it Another Way: Alternative phrases
Brain Work: Test yourself and your memory!

Joke Time

A few years ago Bob Onion was interviewed by a journalist from a local newspaper about the success[1] of the company.
The journalist asked Bob: "How do you find easy answers to problems in the area of production?"
Bob thought for a moment and said: "Normally we hand[2] the problem to the laziest person in the factory. They will find the easiest way to deal with the problem and then we simply use their method."

A person was being interviewed for a job at Onions by the boss of personnel.
Applicant[3]: "Well , I'd like to accept the job but you see in my last job I was paid more money."
Boss: "Yes but they didn't have our fringe benefits[4], did they?"
Applicant: "I had a company car and generous pension[5]".
Boss: "But did you have bonus payments and paid overtime[6]?"
Applicant: "We did. We also had six weeks paid holiday a year".
Boss: "Well, in that case,[7] why did you leave that fantastic company?"
Applicant: "The company went bankrupt[8]".

1 Erfolg 2 weiter-/übergeben 3 Bewerber 4 zusätzliche Leistungen 5 großzügige Rente
6 Überstunden 7 in dem Fall 8 Bankrott machen

Focus: Acknowledging an order

In foreign trade it is normal to send the buyer a written acknowledgement because it can take the goods some time to arrive. Often the seller cannot supply the goods – goods not available from stock – or the seller does not accept the customer's conditions because the discounts or prices are not acceptable. In such cases the seller will usually put forward alternatives, perhaps suggesting a different product or different conditions. This is called a counter – offer.

Dialogue: The Russians wonder how to acknowledge Onions' order

In Pomsk Alex Popov (**AP**) and Vladimir Oblomov (**VO**), owners of a small engineering factory, are very happy. As we know they have received an order from Onions in Birmingham for water pumps. Here they are talking to Alex Mitchel (**AM**), a visiting businessman from Scotland about further business.

AP: Well, Mr Mitchel, our products are selling well in Europe.

AM: Really? That's good news. That's why I'm here too. Maybe we can come to an agreement for distributing your equipment in Britain. My firm could act as your agent and we would deal with all advertising and correspondence.

VO: Correspondence? Oh yes, you mean this letter writing. A big problem for us. We are engineers, not language specialists. And we are not sure about the way you do things. For example, we have an order by post. Is it normal to tell the customer you are dealing with the order? And how? I mean to write and inform them that the order is being produced and when it will be sent? Should you say "Your conditions of business are fine"?

AM: Absolutely. You should tell them you accept the terms ...

AP: Terms?

AM: That means conditions. You should also tell them the goods will arrive on time. You should say things like "We are giving your order priority" and start "Thank you for your order dated ..."

AP: Wonderful. Vladimir do you have a pen and paper and Mr. Mitchel, do you have perhaps five minutes?

Drop Them a Line: A correct acknowledgement

So, after about ten minutes Alex wrote a letter for the Russians to Onions. Here is the letter:

Dear Mr Miller

Thank you very much for your order no. 2493F dated ... for 400 water pumps type T82B. We accept your order at the prices given in your letter as well as the other conditions.
We can confirm that we have sufficient pumps of this type in stock and that the delivery date can be met. As soon as our bank advises us that payment has been arranged, we will organise shipment of the consignment by MS Argus sailing on 12th April from Petersburg due to arrive on 20th April in Liverpool.
We hope that this will be the beginning of a long and successful business relationship and we look forward to hearing from you again soon.

Yours sincerely
A. Popov

Vocabulary: To help you understand

acknowledgement	Auftragsbestätigung
advertise	Werbung machen
advise	(hier) informieren
agent	Vertreter
area	Gebiet
arrive	ankommen
as soon as	so bald wie
available	vorrätig, lieferbar
buyer	Käufer
case	Fall
consignment	Lieferung, Sendung
counter-offer	Gegenangebot
deal with	fertig werden mit
delivery date	Liefertermin
distribute	verteilen

due; the goods are ~ to arrive on the ...	die Waren sollen eintreffen am ...
equipment	Ausrüstung, Geräte
foreign trade	Außenhandel
further	weiter
lazy	faul
look forward to	sich auf etwas freuen
meet; ~ a date	einen Termin einhalten
owner	Besitzer
payment	Zahlung
priority	Vorrang
put forward	vorschlagen
relationship	Beziehung
sail	abfahren
shipment	Sendung, Verschiffung
stock (from stock)	ab Lager
success	Erfolg
successful	erfolgreich
sufficient	ausreichend
suggest	vorschlagen
term	Bedingung

↔ Put It Another Way: Alternative phrases

To start

we thank you for your order placed on ...	wir danken Ihnen für Ihren Auftrag erteilt ... am
many thanks for your order	vielen Dank für Ihren Auftrag

Other details

your goods will be sent/despatched within a few days	Ihre Waren werden in wenigen Tagen abgesandt werden
we will do our best/utmost to complete your order in good time	wir werden uns sehr bemühen, Ihren Auftrag rechtzeitig zu erfüllen

we regret that we cannot supply the goods you ordered	wir bedauern, daß wir nicht in der Lage sind, die von Ihnen bestellten Waren zu liefern
unfortunately we no longer stock this item	leider führen wir diesen Artikel nicht mehr

Ending the letter

we feel certain that you will be satisfied with ...	wir sind sicher, daß Sie mit ... zufrieden sein werden
we hope that this will be the first of many orders	wir hoffen, daß dies der erste von vielen Aufträgen sein wird

B Brain Work Twelve: What's the English for ...?

Okay, over to you. Have a try at the little Brain tests that follow.
Here are some English and German words and phrases from this chapter.
Put the words together.

1) unfortunately	a) einen Artikel führen
2) we feel certain	b) wir bedauern, daß
3) stock an item	c) in wenigen Tagen
4) we will do our utmost	d) rechtzeitig
5) we regret that	e) wir werden uns sehr bemühen
6) in good time	f) leider
7) within a few days	g) wir sind sicher

B Brain Work Thirteen: Put in the missing letters

Here are some words but the secretary was a bit sleepy and missed out a few letters. Your job: identify the words and put in the missing letters.

1) s-ff-ci-nt	2) a-v-se	3) p-y-en-
4) c-nsi-nm-n-	5) s-cce-s-ul	6) d-li-er-

B Brain Work Fourteen: Complete the letter

Oh dear, the secretary was sleepy! Below is a letter with some words missing. To make it a little easier the missing words are in the box. Use the words below (1 to 8) once to make the letter acceptable.

1) to hearing	2) despatch	3) many thanks for	4) regret
5) dated	6) item	7) within	8) no longer

Dear Sir

... (a) ... your order number A251... (b) ... 25th September 19.. for 240 pullovers and 180 sweatshirts.
We... (c) ... that we cannot supply the sweatshirts because we ... (d) ... stock this ... (e) ...
We will ... (f) ... the pullovers ... (g) ... 5 days and look forward ... (h) ... from you again soon.

Yours faithfully

Supply Problems

CONTENTS

Joke Time

Bob Onion was visiting Gerry Murry who was in hospital with a broken leg[1]. Onion said: "Don't worry[2] Gerry, everybody at work is ready to cover for[3] you while you are off work."
"Oh, that's good!" said Gerry.
"Yes, as soon as we know what you have been doing!"

Onions is an expanding[4] firm. A new factory had to be built. One day while it was being constructed Bob Onion arrived to look at the situation. He was happy until he got into his Rolls and found he had no petrol in the tank[5].
"Could you give the car a push up the hill?" he asked a builder.
"I think so" said the helpful young man.
After about ten minutes the car arrived at a garage. The young man was in a terrible condition, red in the face, sweating,[6] and gasping for breath[7].
Onion had the tank filled up and then said to the red faced worker, "Thanks a lot. Do you smoke?"
The young man expecting a box of expensive cigars said " Oh yes, I do!"
"Well if I were you I would stop. You are clearly not fit." Then he drove away.

1 gebrochenes Bein 2 keine Sorge 3 einspringen für 4 wachsend 5 kein Benzin im Tank
6 schwitzend 7 nach Atem ringend

Focus: Problems with supply and delivery

When buyer and supplier have agreed on conditions the supplier then must deliver the goods. The delivery is usually organised by the seller. Small, light items can be sent by post. For larger orders a forwarding agent is normally used. Often the buyer will ask for a despatch advice which says when the goods have been shipped. There are many reasons why an order cannot be executed. In this case a supplier should inform the buyer of the reasons for a delay or other problems.

Dialogue: Strikes and troubles for Onions

At Onions there have been one or two problems in the factory. The union has decided that overtime on Sundays should be double normal pay. At the moment Onions is very successful and the order books are so full that the factory is working at full capacity, and to execute all orders for heating equipment there is work on Saturdays and Sundays. Ian Burns (**IB**), the new head of personnel is talking to the shop steward, Mick Lake (**ML**).

ML: Business is very good. We are doing a lot of overtime at the moment and we want more pay for it.
IB: Yes, but we must be competitive. Look at those other firms that have not cut their costs. They have gone bankrupt. No job at all!
ML: Well, if you don't offer more money I'm afraid we'll work to rule and there may be a go slow.
IB: What, industrial action? We will lose orders and you'll lose jobs.
ML: The members of the union have decided to take industrial action until Onions sees reason!

Later Ian Burns talks to Bob Onion (**BO**).

BO: So it looks like we'll have delays in orders and perhaps some cancellations. Damn it Burns, we Onions have sold boilers for years and never had any trouble with unions. Onions and unions have never had problems. That is until I hired university types and had a personnel department!

IB: At the moment the union is not doing overtime. It will clearly hold up orders.

BO: Do something, Burns! Fire somebody, that's what I pay you for!

IB: It just isn't as simple as that. We'll have to tell our customers that we have problems. A few letters must be written.

BO: If this goes on much longer you will be writing a few letters, letters of application!

Drop Them a Line: Delivery time cannot be met

We have seen that Onions have got production problems. Here is one of a lot of letters sent out that week to customers:

Dear Sir

We very much regret to inform you that we are forced to ask for an extension of time in the execution of your order no. E560 placed on 16th March. Industrial action at our plant in Birmingham has resulted in a delay in despatching some orders. However,we believe that we can carry out delivery within a week. We apologise for the delay and hope you have understanding for our difficulties and please be assured that we are doing all we can to make the delivery on time.
As you requested we will advise you as soon as the order is ready for shipment.

Yours faithfully

(V) Vocabulary: To help you understand

apologise	sich entschuldigen
assure somebody	jemandem versichern
buyer	Käufer
cancellation	Stornierung
carry out	ausführen
competitive	konkurrenzfähig
cover for	einspringen für
cut the costs	die Kosten reduzieren
delay	Verspätung
delivery time	Lieferzeit
despatch	senden
despatch advice	Versandanzeige
don't worry	keine Sorge
execute orders	Bestellungen ausführen
execution	Ausführung
extension	Verlängerung
force; ~ somebody to do something	jemanden zwingen, etwas zu tun
forwarding agent	Spediteur
go slow	Bummelstreik
goods	Waren
hold up	verspäten, Verspätung
in this case	in diesem Fall
industrial action	Arbeitskampfmaßnahmen
order book	Auftragsbuch
overtime	Überstunden
plant	Fabrik
reason	Vernunft, Grund
request	bitten, ersuchen
result in	führen zu
ship	versenden, verschiffen
shop steward	Arbeitnehmervertreter
union	Gewerkschaft
work to rule	Dienst nach Vorschrift

↔ Put It Another Way: Alternative phrases

To start

we are really/indeed sorry	wir bedauern wirklich
please accept our apologies for	bitte nehmen Sie unsere Entschuldigung entgegen
we regret to have to tell you that ...	wir bedauern, Ihnen mitteilen zu müssen, daß ...

Reasons for the delay

demand was so great that ...	Nachfrage war so groß, daß ...
our stock has been exhausted/ used up	unsere Vorräte sind erschöpft
a fire damaged our plant	ein Feuer hat unsere Fabrik beschädigt
our suppliers found it impossible to keep pace with orders	unsere Lieferanten waren nicht imstande, mit den Aufträgen Schritt zu halten
an unexpected shortage of raw materials	eine unerwartete Rohstoffknappheit

Ending the letter

we hope that you will appreciate/ understand our position	wir hoffen, daß Sie unsere Lage verstehen
we hope that this delay will not cause you considerable inconvenience	wir hoffen, daß diese Verzögerung Ihnen keine wesentlichen Unannehmlichkeiten verursacht
we wish to assure that we are doing everything to despatch your order	wir möchten Ihnen versichern, daß wir alles tun, Ihren Auftrag auf den Weg zu bringen

B Brain Work Fifteen: What's the English for ...?

One of your colleagues has written some sentences but they did not know all the words in English. You know the words so help your colleague and change the German words for English ones.

1) This firm is not *konkurrenzfähig.*
2) We will *senden* the goods within 5 days.
3) We want to *uns entschuldigen* for the delay in the *Ausführung* of your order.
4) Industrial action resulted in a *Verspätung*.
5) *Auftragsbücher* are so full that the workers are doing *Überstunden.*
6) We are *gezwungen* to ask for an extension of the delivery time.

B Brain Work Sixteen: A little letter writing

This time please put the words below into the letter.

despatch	assure	position	damaged
delay	sorry	executing	

Dear Mrs Duffy

We are really ... (1) ... to inform you that there will be a delay in ... (2) ... your order
number F1644 placed on 1st June of this year.
The reason for the ... (3) ... is that a fire ... (4) .... our factory last week. We hope you understand our ... (5) ... and we wish to ... (6) ... you that we are doing everything to ... (7) ... your order within 14 days.

Yours sincerely

R. Ahonen

B Brain Work Seventeen: Quiz time

Okay, let's see what you can remember. Ready? Good luck!
Circle one letter for the correct answer.

1) "A cancellation of an order" means:

a) the order will be late
b) the order will be early
c) there will be no order

2) "Despatch an order" means:

a) to send the order
b) to put the order in boxes
c) to repair the goods

3) A plant is another word for:

a) a factory
b) a sort of office
c) a sort of strike

4) "The strike will hold up delivery" means:

a) delivery will be by air
b) delivery will be late
c) delivery will be sent now

5) To apologise means:

a) to say hello
b) to say sorry
c) to deliver

6) To request is another way to say:

a) to ask for
b) to do again
c) to carry out

7 Chapter

Payment

CONTENTS

Focus: Payment overseas and how it is done
Dialogue: The head of sales learns a few things
Drop Them a Line: Arranging payment
Put It Another Way: Alternative phrases
Brain Work: 'What's the English for?'
and some other tests

Joke Time

Bob Unwin decided to hire a chauffeur from an agency to drive his Rolls.
On the first morning Bob Unwin asked him, " Driver, what's your name?"
"George, sir," replied[1] the chauffeur.
"I don't call my drivers by their first name! What's your second name?"
"Well, it's Darling, sir"
"In that case, drive on George" said Unwin.

1 antwortete

Focus: How to pay bills abroad

Paying for products at home is a simple matter. We can pay in advance or after delivery. Payment is normally by cheque, draft or transfer. There can be problems if the buyer does not want to or cannot pay. In foreign trade these problems are greater. There is a lot of correspondence and the seller must wait months for payment, the buyer must wait months for the goods. Banks are very important here because they help to collect payment, handle shipping documents and act as agents for foreign banks. They also guarantee conditions of payment. Payment for foreign trade is usually made by banker's transfer, letter of credit or bill of exchange.

Dialogue: The head of sales learns a few things

Tom Parker (**TP**) is the head of sales at Onions. He is talking to Sally Benson (**SB**) in finance about paying customers abroad and more important about being paid.

TP: You see Sally, I've been with Onions for 20 years. Most of the time we've done business with companies in Britain, we've hardly sold anything abroad, you know, to foreign companies.

SB: Things change, Tom. We must be flexible and we need to expand. We must sell and buy outside Britain if we want to stay in business.

TP: It's all so complicated. I mean in Britain, for example, if I wanted parts from Potters Ltd, I just wrote them a cheque or transferred the money to their account. Simple, no problem.

SB: Yes, but you can't do that with a company 5,000 miles away, maybe in India. Sellers can't be sure they'll get their money and buyers can't be sure they'll get their goods.

TP: That's the problem! Precisely.

SB: It's not a problem if, for example, you use a letter of credit. Let's say that we want to buy components worth £500 from a company in Korea. We ask our bank to issue a letter of credit for £500 in favour of the seller. There is a special form for this. It contains all the conditions of the transaction agreed by us and the firm in Korea.

Then, our bank sends these instructions to its agent in Korea. In this case the agent is a bank. The bank in Korea contacts the sellers and advises them of the credit. Now this is very safe.

TP: Why's that?

SB: Because the agent bank will pay the sellers if the conditions on the letter are fulfilled, so the sellers can execute our order and know they will be paid. We are happy because the agent bank only pays if we get our goods according to the order.

TP: I'm still not totally clear ...

SB: Look at these letters ...

Drop Them a Line: Arranging payment

Here is a letter written to Onions by Arumco in Saudi Arabia with an order for special industrial heating units for a chemical process.

Dear Sirs

Thank you for your letter dated 18th March 19.. enclosing your terms and catalogue. We wish to place the attached order and would appreciate prompt execution.
We have instructed The El Turkiy National Bank Damman to open a credit for £8,540 in your favour, valid until 30th June 19.. . The credit will be confirmed by their agent bank The G.I.F Bank, 27 Booker street, Birmingham T48SOW who will accept your draft on them for the amount of your invoice for 60 days.
Please attach the following documents to your draft:

Insurance policy for £9,000
2 commercial invoices
2 bills of lading

Please advise us when the units have been despatched.

Yours faithfully

Mohamed Al Baab

Onions sent a reply to the above letter:

Dear Mr Al Baab

We were very happy to receive your order and can confirm that the units you request are in stock.
We agree to your method of payment and note that it is by irrevocable letter of credit for a sum not in excess of £8,540 valid until 30th June 19..
As soon as we receive confirmation of this credit from The G.I.F. Bank in Birmingham, we shall despatch your order.
We assure you that your order is being given prompt attention and that the units ordered by you are of the best quality.

Yours sincerely

Frank Howard

(V) Vocabulary: To help you understand

abroad	im Ausland
accept a draft	eine Tratte mit einem Akzept versehen
according to	entsprechend
act as an agent	als Agent arbeiten
advance; in ~	im voraus
advise	benachrichtigen
agency	Agentur
amount	Betrag
attach	beiheften
bill	Rechnung
bill of exchange	übertragbare Zahlungsanweisung, Wechsel
bill of lading	Seefrachtbrief / Konnossement
collect payment	einziehen, Inkasso durchführen
commercial invoice	Handelsrechnung
condition of payment	Zahlungsbedingung
confirm	bestätigen

contain	enthalten
darling	Schatz, Liebling
decide	entscheiden; sich ~
draft	Tratte, gezogener Wechsel
excess; in ~ of	übersteigen
execute	ausführen
execution	Ausführung
favour; in your favour ~	zu Ihren Gunsten
foreign trade	Außenhandel
form	Formular
fulfil	erfüllen
handle	bearbeiten
head	Leiter
instruct, instruction	anweisen, Anweisung
insurance policy	Versicherungspolice
invoice	Warenrechnung
irrevocable letter of credit	unwiderrufliches Akkreditiv
issue a letter of credit	ein Akkreditiv ausstellen
letter of credit	Akkreditiv, Kreditbrief
matter	Sache
note	zur Kenntnis nehmen
shipping documents	Versanddokumente
transaction	Geschäft, Transaktion, Abwicklung
transfer	überweisen, Überweisung
valid until	gültig bis

↔ Put It Another Way: Alternative phrases

we have arranged payment through the N.I.T. Bank for the amount of ...	wir haben Zahlung in Höhe von ... durch die N.I.T. Bank vorgenommen
we have transferred the amount to your account	wir haben auf Ihr Konto den Betrag überwiesen

cash on delivery /COD	per Nachnahme
cash in advance	Vorauszahlung
I thank you for your delivery and I enclose a cheque covering the amount of your invoice.	ich danke Ihnen für Ihre Lieferung und füge einen Scheck über den Rechnungsbetrag bei
the goods arrived in good condition	die Waren sind in gutem Zustand angekommen

B Brain Work Eighteen: What's the English for ...?

To give you a little brain exercise put together the English and German words.

1) advise	a) zur Kenntnis nehmen
2) note	b) bestätigen
3) fulfil	c) benachrichtigen
4) attach	d) erfüllen
5) execute	e) ausführen
6) confirm	f) beiheften

B Brain Work Nineteen: Complete the sentences

Test yourself a little more and please complete these sentences with the words below. Use each word once. Use the first letter in this chapter to help you. Please note, there is an extra word!

confirmed valid execute favour instructed attach

1) Please ... shipping documents
2) We have ... our bank in Tobago to open a letter of credit in your ...
3) Please ... the order promptly.
4) The credit is ... until 15th april 19.. .
5) The letter of credit will be ... by their agent bank in Stockholm.

B Brain Work Twenty: Letter writing

Your chance to use what you have learned in this chapter! Here is a letter discussing payment. Please put in the words below to complete the letter.

confirmed	enclosing	instructed	agent
valid	irrevocable	open	

Dear Sir

Many thanks for your letter of 20th June 19.. ... (1) ... your terms and information about the radios and television sets produced by your firm. We wish to place an order.

We have ... (2) ... our bank, The International Finance Bank Durban, to ... (3) ... an ... (4) ... letter of credit for US$ 1,850 in your favour ... (5) ... until 20th September. The credit will be ... (6) ... by their ... (7) ... bank in London,
The PLS Bank, 32 Queensbury rd., LONDON SW4 3G1 who will accept your draft on them for the amount of your invoice.

Yours faithfully

B Brain Work Twenty One: True or false?

This is another bit of brain work but see how you do and then have a rest! From the text on payment decide which of the statements below are true or false.

1) It is more complex paying for products at home. T / F
2) Sellers must wait longer for payment with foreign trade. T / F
3) Banks are important in foreign trade. T / F
4) Bills of exchange and letters of credit are not used in foreign trade. T / F

Delays In Payment, Part One

CONTENTS

Focus: Delays in payment – asking for your money!
Dialogue: A telephone call to ask about payment
Drop Them a Line: A follow-up to the phone call
Put It another Way: Alternative phrases
Brain Work: Correcting a letter and a little quiz

Joke Time

A customer phones Gerry Murry's secretary in the sales department at Onions.
Customer: I'd like to talk to Mr Murry, please.
Secretary: I'm very sorry but he's not in this afternoon.
Customer: Well, this is the third time I've tried to reach him! Doesn't he work in the afternoon?
Secretary: Oh no, you are wrong. Actually he doesn't work in the morning. He just doesn't come in the office in the afternoon.

Focus: Delays in payment – asking for your money!

Sometimes a customer will not pay on time. In this case you should not think that she or he does not intend to pay. There could be a number of reasons why the account is overdue. Perhaps the customer did not receive your bill or the bill has been overlooked. Maybe there has been a problem with payment, a lost cheque in the post, a misunderstanding at the bank. So the first letter should be a polite enquiry asking about the delay. If the customer ignores the first letter or acknowledges it but still does not pay you should write a second letter. This letter should be a little more firm. You should refer to the previous letter and send copies of relevant bills. The third request or final demand should review the situation so far, saying you have been patient, and telling the customer what action you will take. Do not threaten legal action unless you intend to take it!

Dialogue: A telephone call to ask about payment

Susan Wright (**SW**), a member of the sales department at Onions, telephones a building company to ask why they have not paid a bill for heating equipment (**S: secretary**).

S: Hello, Melmoths the builders. Can I help you?

SW: Good morning, my name is Susan Wright and I'm phoning about some heating equipment your firm ordered from us two months ago. Can I speak to Mr Melmoth, please?

S: Oh, er, he's away at the moment.

SW: Will he be away long?

S: I'm not sure actually, you see he's been rather ill and ...

SW: Well, maybe you could help.You see we haven't been paid for ...

S: Oh, I don't think I can help you there. I'm only temporary, standing in and answering the phone. Could you write a letter and I'll see that Mr Melmoth gets it?

SW: Well, okay. You'll get the letter in a few days.

Drop Them a Line: A follow-up to the phone call

The golden rule is always to have something on paper!
So after the telephone conversation Susan Wright writes a letter to Melmoths reminding the firm about the overdue bill:

Dear Mr Melmoth

As you normally clear your accounts promptly we think you may have overlooked our invoice No 7D 34 for £453.75 which was due six weeks ago. Could you please let us have your cheque to clear the bill?
However, if you have already sent a remittance, please disregard this letter.
Attached please find a copy of the bill.
We look forward to hearing from you soon.

Yours sincerely

Vocabulary: To help you understand

account	Rechnung, Konto
acknowledgement	Bestätigung
attached	beigeheftet, beiliegend
builder	Bauunternehmer
clear a bill	begleichen; eine Rechnung ~
delay	Verspätung, Verzögerung
disregard	ignorieren, nicht beachten
due	fällig
enquiry	Anfrage
final demand	letzte Mahnung
firm	bestimmt, fest
heating equipment	Heizgerät
intend	beabsichtigen
invoice	Warenrechnung
legal action	Klage
member	Mitglied

misunderstanding	Mißverständnis
on time	pünktlich
overdue	überfällig
overlook	übersehen
previous	vorhergehend, früher
reason	Grund
refer to	sich beziehen auf
remind somebody of	erinnern; jemanden ~ an
remittance	Zahlung
request	Bitte
settle a bill	begleichen
settlement	Bezahlung
stand in	einspringen, vertreten
temporary	vorübergehend
threaten	drohen

↔ Put It Another Way: Alternative phrases

Starting a letter

we should like to remind you that ...	wir möchten Sie daran erinnern, daß ...
we are sorry to inform you that...	es tut uns leid, Ihnen mitteilen zu müssen, daß ...
may we remind you that ...	dürfen wir Sie daran erinnern, daß ...
we wish to draw your attention to ...	wir möchten Sie auf ... aufmerksam machen

Requests for payment

we would appreciate it if you sent us payment promptly	wir würden uns freuen, wenn Sie uns den Rechnungsbetrag bald zukommen ließen
payment is now four weeks overdue	die Zahlung ist jetzt vier Wochen überfällig

an early settlement of your account would be appreciated	eine baldige Begleichung Ihrer Rechnung würden wir begrüßen
we must point out that your bill is still outstanding	wir machen Sie darauf aufmerksam, daß Ihre Rechnung noch ausstehend ist

Ending a letter

will you please let us have ...	bitte, schicken Sie uns ...
we look forward to receiving ...	wir freuen uns, ... zu erhalten
we trust that you will clear your account in the next few days	wir hoffen, daß Sie Ihre Rechnung in den nächsten Tagen begleichen werden

B Brain Work Twenty Two: Over to you – letter writing

Oh dear, the letter you wrote on the computer is mixed up. There must be a problem with the program! Well, now you must sort out the sentences and put them in the best order.

1) We look forward to hearing from you in the next few days.
2) Dear Mr Free
3) An early settlement of this account would be appreciated.
4) Please find a copy of your invoice attached.
5) Yours sincerely
6) We should like to remind you that payment for order No 439B is a month overdue.
7) If you have already sent a remittance please disregard this letter.

Ⓑ Brain Work Twenty Three: A little quiz – true or false

From the Focus on Delays in Payment decide which of the questions below are true or false.

1) You should always threaten legal action in the first letter. T / F
2) The second letter is also called the final demand. T / F
3) Customers sometimes overlook bills. T / F
4) The word 'overdue' means late. T / F
5) You should send original bills to customers. T / F

Ⓑ Brain Work Twenty Four: What's the English for ...?

Oh no! Your colleague has tried to write another letter but could not remember the English for some words. The result is that there are some German words in these sentences from the letter. Use the information in this chapter to help you put the German words into English.

1) Payment was *fällig* a month ago.
2) Could you please *begleichen* your account as soon as possible?
3) Please *ignorieren* this letter if you have already cleared the account.
4) Thank you for the *Zahlung* of the bill.
5) The *Warenrechnung* has not yet been paid.
6) Please see the *beigeheftete* account.

Delays In Payment, Part Two

CONTENTS

Joke Time

An employee[1] went to see Bob Onion.
Employee: Excuse me, sir, but I've been working here for over ten years and doing the work of three men. I think it's time I had a rise.

Bob Onion: Well, I must think about giving you a rise but there is no problem about these three men. Give me their names and I'll fire them!

The office boy turned up[2] half an hour late one morning and the boss said, "You should have been here at nine o'clock!"
The office boy looked at the boss and said, "Why, what happened?[3]"

1 Arbeitnehmer, Angestellte 2 auftauchen 3 passieren

Focus: Delays in payment – final demands

As we saw in the last chapter, if a customer does not pay on time the seller should write a polite letter enquiring about the delay. If, however, there is no reply or no payment the seller should write again including copies of invoices. Finally, if after the second letter there is still no reply or payment a final demand is sent often giving a last date or deadline. After this time the seller will take some kind of action to get the payment.

Dialogue: Discussing further steps

Susan Wright (**SW**) from Sales and the trainee, Terry Jones (**TJ**), are looking at the accounts.

SW: Well, it looks like we need to write to a couple of customers.
TJ: Why? What's wrong?
SW: Some of them just won't pay unless you say things like "We are forced to put the matter in the hands of our solicitor", or "We shall be compelled to take legal proceedings against you."
TJ: What does that mean exactly, pay up or you are in trouble?
SW: In a very simple way, yes. Some people just don't take things seriously unless you threaten them with legal action. That's what I'm going to do with this firm of builders, Melmoths.

Drop them a Line: Onions' final demand to Melmoths

Onions already phoned and wrote to Melmoths ,the builders, but they did not receive an answer or payment so Sue Wright writes the following letter – a final demand:

Dear Mr Melmoth

We have written to you on two occasions, 14th September and 21st November, concerning the outstanding balance for order No 7D34 of £475.75.
We had expected that you would have settled the matter by now but

you have offered no explanation for the delay and sent no remittance. Regrettably, unless we receive payment within the next seven days we will be forced to put the matter in the hands of our solicitor.

Yours sincerely

S. Wright

(V) Vocabulary: To help you understand

account	Rechnung
balance	Kontostand, Saldo; begleichen
concerning	bezüglich, hinsichtlich
compel	zwingen
couple of	ein paar
deadline	letzter Termin
delay	Verzögerung, Verspätung
enquire	fragen, erkundigen
explanation	Erklärung
final demand	letzte Mahnung
finally	endlich
force	zwingen
however	jedoch
include	einschließen
legal proceedings	Verfahren, Gerichtsverhandlung
matter	Sache
occasion	Gelegenheit, Anlaß
offer	anbieten
outstanding	ausstehend
pay up	zurückzahlen
polite	höflich
rent	Miete
rise	Erhöhung (Geld)
regrettably	bedauerlicherweise

remittance	Zahlung
reply	Antwort
settle	erledigen
solicitor	Anwalt
spare parts	Ersatzteile
threaten	drohen
unless	es sei denn, wenn nicht
wrong (what's wrong?)	was ist los?

↔ Put it Another Way: Alternative phrases

Starting the letter

we are at a loss to understand why ...	wir können nicht verstehen, warum ...
we note with regret that ...	wir stellen mit Bedauern fest, daß ...
we regret that we ...	wir bedauern, daß wir ...
inspite of two reminders...	trotz zweier Mahnungen
we have written to you a number of times	wir haben Ihnen mehrmals geschrieben

Making your point!

we must insist on payment	wir müssen auf Zahlung bestehen
the account is now three months overdue	die Rechnung ist jetzt drei Monate überfällig
we have no alternative but to ...	uns bleibt nichts anderes übrig, als ...
unless we hear from you within seven days ...	wenn wir innerhalb der nächsten sieben Tage ... nichts von Ihnen hören

we will instruct our solicitors to start proceedings against you	wir werden unsere Rechtsanwälte anweisen, gerichtliche Schritte gegen Sie einzuleiten
if your cheque fails to arrive within ...	falls Ihr Scheck nicht innerhalb ... eintrifft

Ending the letter

please pay the account and settle this matter without further delay	begleichen Sie bitte die Rechnung ohne weitere Verzögerung
we hope that you will deal with this matter as soon as possible	wir hoffen, daß Sie diese Angelegenheit so bald wie möglich erledigen

B Brain Work Twenty Five: Complete the letter

Here is a chance to see what you can remember. Below are some words and phrases. Use each one once to complete the sentences.

regrettably insist outstanding solicitor remittance reminders

1) In spite of two ... you have still not settled your account.
2) We must ... on payment within seven days.
3) We will put the matter in the hands of our ....
4) ..., if your cheque fails to arrive tomorrow, we will be forced to instruct our solicitors to start proceedings against you.
5) Your account has been ... for three months.
6) We look forward to receiving your ... next week.

B Brain Work Twenty Six: What's the English for ...?

Here are some English words with letters missing. Please add the letters to complete the word. The German for the words is below to help you but not in the correct order!

bezüglich Zahlung es sei denn ausstehend Verzögerung

1) r-mitt-nc- 2) -onc-rni-g 3) d-l-y 4) o-tst-ndi-ng 5) u-le-s

Now put the English word and German word together.

B Brain Work Twenty Seven: Quiz time

Have a try at this little quiz. Good luck! Circle one letter for the correct answer.

1) A "remittance" is an alternative word for

a) delay
b) payment
c) letter

2) A third letter asking for payment is also called

a) an invoice
b) a final demand
c) a last request

3) An "outstanding account"is

a) a very positive bank balance
b) a bill that is not paid
c) a cheque sent by post

4) If you "attach" a copy to a letter you

a) send the copy separately
b) fix the copy to the letter
c) fax the copy with the letter

Letter Box: By and until

Most people have problems with "by" and "until". This is because in German both words can be translated by "bis". Look at the two sentences below to see the diference.

1) I will be in Paris until Tuesday.
2) I will be in Paris by Tuesday (at the latest).

Sentence 1) means that I am in Paris at the moment and I will leave on Tuesday.

Sentence 2) means I am not in Paris at the moment but I will be in Paris on Saturday, Sunday or anytime before or on Tuesday. I will be in Paris on Tuesday at the latest.

Note the sentences:

1) We will make payment until 1st January.
2) We will make payment by 1st January (at the latest).

Sentence 1) means several payments are made, the last one on 1st January.

Sentence 2) means one payment made between now and 1st January.

To help you remember the difference note that the "mindestens haltbar" sign on food is called "use/sell by date" in English. You can only use a litre of milk one time before the date. You cannot drink the milk again and again! As another tip, ask yourself is the action one time (by) or several, continual actions (until)?

B Brain Work Twenty Eight: A little work on "by" and "until"

Okay, let's see if you can see the diference between by and until. In the sentences put in until or by. Remember that you can say at the latest (spätestens) with by.

1) I will arrive at the airport ... 7o'clock. My flight is at 9.25.
2) I will be on the train ... 10.40. I arrive in London at 10.40.
3) We will supply spare parts ... you sell the machine.
4) The rent must be paid ... the first of the month.
5) Please pay the remittance ... the end of the week.

Apologies

CONTENTS

Focus: Apologies
Dialogue: John Melmoth finds out what went wrong
Drop Them a Line: Melmoth says sorry to Onions
Put It Another Way: Alternative phrases
Brain Work: Complete a letter and test your memory

Joke Time

In Onions the boss of the sales department asked the new junior[1]:
"Have you posted those two things I gave you, you know, the letter to Sydney and that little parcel of components[2] to Manchester?"
"I have", said the junior full of pride[3]," and what's more, I put right that mistake you made with the postage."
"How do you mean?" said the boss surprised.
"Well, you put £8.20 worth of stamps on the local parcel and only a stamp for 80p on that letter to Australia. Don't worry, I sorted it out[4].
I just changed the addresses."

1 Büroaushilfe 2 Komponenten 3 Stolz 4 erledigen

Focus: Apologies – saying sorry

It sometimes happens that in business you will need to say sorry and explain a difficult situation. If there is a delay in payment, for example, you should write to the supplier and give reasons for the hold up. Perhaps you can make alternative suggestions about payment or the supply of a product. This is simple courtesy.
Do not forget that the people you are doing business with have debts and deadlines too. Also, do not forget that it is good business practice. Maybe you will need to do business with this firm again. Even if you do not, you will do business with another firm and 'word gets around'. It is not good for your business if people think you are unreliable.

Dialogue: John Melmoth finds out what went wrong

The boss of Melmoths, John Melmoth (**JM**), comes back to the office after being away for three months. He left his son, Kevin (**KM**), in charge.

JM: A final demand from Onions? Good grief! Why didn't you pay the bill before?
KM: We've had a few problems keeping up with the correspondence side. Sandra left two months ago and we had trouble finding another secretary, so, you know Marvin's sister, nice girl, well, she had a go at the job.
JM: Had a go! You mean Marvin who works for us? His sister? Well, if she's as smart as he is I expect that letters were badly typed, replies lost, faxes sent to wrong place ...
KM: Well, don't worry, she didn't do that, in fact she didn't do anything. She left after two days.
JM: And then what?
KM: We hired a girl from the agency. She seemed very good until we found out how she dealt with the correspondence. One evening I moved a filing cabinet from the office and found all these letters behind it.
JM: So you fired her!
KM: That's right. We got another secretary, from a different agency, but she left ...

JM: After a week?
KM: After one morning, trying to sort out the mess the other girl made.
JM: Well, it looks like I've got some letter writing, phoning and thinking up excuses to do!

Drop them a Line: Melmoths say sorry to Onions

John Melmoth thought about what he would say. After a while he puts pen to paper and writes a letter to Onions explaining why they have not received a bill:

Dear Mrs Wright
We were indeed very sorry to receive your final demand for our order No 7D34 for the amount of £475.75.
The cause of the considerable delay was due entirely to circumstances beyond our control.
I enclose a cheque for the amount and very much regret the inconvenience this delay has caused you. I also hope that this delay will not have a negative effect on our future business relationship and assure you that delays will not occur in future.

Yours sincerely
J. Melmoth.

Vocabulary: To help you understand

agency	Agentur
amount	Betrag
assure; ~ somebody of something	jemanden etwas versichern
beyond our control	nicht in unserer Hand liegend
business practice	Geschäftspraxis
business relationship	Geschäftsbeziehung
cause	verursachen/Ursache
charge; in ~	verantwortlich

circumstance	Umstand
considerable	groß, erheblich
courtesy	Höflichkeit
debts	Schulden
due to	infolge
entirely	völlig
excuse	Ausrede
explain	erklären
filing cabinet	Aktenschrank
future	Zukunft
good grief!	Mein Gott!
have a go at something	versuchen, etwas zu tun
have trouble	Probleme haben
hire	einstellen
hold up	Verzögerung, Verspätung
inconvenience	Unannehmlichkeit
junior	Bürogehilfe
keep up with	Schritt halten mit
occur	vorkommen
postage	Porto
pride	Stolz
reply/replies	Antwort/en
sales department	Verkaufsabteilung
sort out	erledigen
suggestion	Vorschlag
supplier	Lieferant
surprised	überrascht
think up	erfinden, ausdenken
unreliable	unzuverlässig
word gets round that ...	man munkelt, daß ...

↔ Put It Another Way: Alternative phrases

Starting a letter

we very much regret	wir bedauern sehr
please accept our apologies for	wir bitten um Entschuldigung wegen
we are extremely sorry	es tut uns äußerst leid

Reasons for delay

business has been slack	das Geschäft geht schlecht
we are in difficulties as our main customer has gone bankrupt	wir sind in Schwierigkeiten gekommen, weil unser Hauptkunde Konkurs gemacht hat
our customers have recently been slow in meeting their obligations	unsere Kunden kommen in der letzten Zeit ihren Verpflichtungen schleppend nach
our present problems are only temporary	unsere gegenwärtigen Schwierigkeiten sind nur vorübergehend
we are experiencing great difficulty in collecting payment	wir haben erhebliche Schwierigkeiten beim Einzug unserer Rechnungen

Promising payment

you will find enclosed a cheque for £12.50 in full settlement of your bill	wir fügen einen Scheck über £12.50 zum vollen Ausgleich Ihrer Rechnung bei
we will clear the outstanding amount by the end of this month	wir werden die ausstehende Summe bis Ende dieses Monats begleichen
please be good enough to grant us a few weeks in which to pay	bitte seien Sie so freundlich und gewähren Sie uns noch einige Wochen zur Zahlung
we are making every effort to pay the bill by the end of November	wir werden alle Anstrengungen unternehmen, um die Rechnung bis Ende November zu bezahlen

we have today instructed our bank	heute haben wir unsere Bank angewiesen
to transfer £58 to your account	£58 auf Ihr Konto zu überweisen

B Brain Work Twenty Nine: What's the English for ...?

Now you can put the English word together with the German word.

1) inconvenience	a) Antwort
2) occur	b) Verzögerung
3) hold up	c) Unannehmlichkeit
4) assure	d) vorkommen
5) considerable	e) versichern
6) reply	f) groß, erheblich

B Brain Work Thirty: Complete the sentences

Time for you to see what you remember. Use the words below to complete the sentences. Use each word only once.

assure   enclose   inconvenience   beyond   receive

1) We were very sorry to ... your final demand.
2) The cause of the delay was ... our control.
3) We ... a cheque for the amount.
4) We also regret the ... this delay has caused you.
5) I wish to ... you that this delay in payment will not occur again.

B Brain Work Thirty One: A little translating

Here is a letter explaining the reason for a delay and asking for more time to pay. The letter is in English but some of the words are in German. Please put the words in English. Use the phrases from this chapter to help you.

Dear Sir

Wir bedauern sehr the delay in payment of your *Rechnung* No B527 for £102.50.
The reason for the *Verzögerung* is that *wir in Schwierigkeiten gekommen sind* because our *Kunden kommen in der letzten Zeit ihren Verpflichtungen schleppend nach.*
We *versichern* you that our *gegenwärtige Schwierigkeiten* are only *vorübergehend* and we will clear the *ausstehende* amount *bis Ende dieses Monats.*

Yours faithfully

Delays in Delivery

CONTENTS

Joke Time

Back at Onions, in Bob Onion's Office:
Secretary: Excuse me, Mr Onion, but I think that somebody wants to talk to you on the phone.
Bob Onion: Now, what on earth does that mean, young woman? Listen, does somebody want to speak to me or not? You think that somebody wants to talk to me?
Secretary: Well, Mr Onion, all I can say is that the caller asked if the 'senile old fool' was in the office, so I wasn't sure if you wanted to take it.

Focus: Delays in delivery – breaking a contract

Clearly, if a supplier is late delivering goods or does not deliver the goods at all he/she has broken a contract. This is called a breach of contract. Here is an example letter for the worst case:

Dear Sirs

The long delays in the execution of your orders is of great concern to us. Over the past months we have contacted you concerning delays and you have made various promises to us. In good faith we have informed our customers that goods would arrive in good time. In virtually every case you have let us down and as a consequence our customers no longer believe us.
As a result of this failure to deliver on time or at all, a number of our best customers are cancelling orders. We estimate that we have already lost £40,000 of cancelled orders due to your inability to deliver as agreed. This is an extremely unsatisfactory situation as it has led to a loss, not only of business, but also confidence in ourselves.You may be assured this will have serious results for our company and yours.

Yours faithfully

Dialogue: Singapore is late with a delivery to Onions

At the purchasing department in Onions the production manager, Nick James (**NJ**), is discussing a delay in the delivery with one of the buyers, Sue Weakly (**SW**).

NJ: What's the problem with the electric motors we ordered from that firm in Singapore? We only have about twenty left in stock and we will need fifty for that new order.

SW: Well, we have not done much business with them before. We used to get 70% of our motors from Britain and the rest from Germany.

NJ: Yes, and who decided to place an order with a firm in Singapore?

SW: Actually, I decided to do it because the British firms could not produce enough and on time and the German firm was too expensive. Anyway I have already written to them. Here's the letter.

NJ: Yes, but at least the German firm was reliable. Well, hopefully we'll get a reply or the motors next week. You know that all this sending letters is very fine but we need the motors.

Drop Them a Line: Onions complain about the delay

Sue Weakly wrote to the Singapore company and here is the letter:

Dear Mr Wung

On 14th June we placed an order for 120 electric motors type M200 produced by you (order No A564).
You assured us that you could supply the motors from stock and we would receive them within eight weeks. Nine weeks have now passed and we are still not in receipt of the consignment.
As we pointed out when we ordered, a prompt delivery was essential. Since we require the motors urgently we regret that we shall be compelled to cancel the order if the shipment does not arrive by the end of the month.

Yours sincerely
S. Weakly

Shortly after Onions received a fax:

Fax to: S Weakly, Purchasing; Onion Engineering 0044 121/345655
Fax from: T Wung Date 07.08.9.

Dear Sir

Very sorry about overdue shipment of motors. We are pleased to report the goods were shipped on the SS Voyager on 20th June. Our shipping agent informs us that due to bad weather the ship was delayed for a week. He assures us that you will receive your goods within the week.

Yours sincerely
T Wung.

(V) Vocabulary: To help you understand

agreed	vereinbart
anyway	trotzdem
assume	annehmen
at all	überhaupt
at least	mindestens
believe	glauben
breach of contract	Vertragsbruch
caller	Anrufer
cancel	stornieren
clearly	offensichtlich
compel	zwingen
concern	Sorge, Besorgnis
concerning	bezüglich
confidence	Vertrauen
consequence	Folge
consignment	Sendung
contract	Vertrag
do business	Geschäfte machen
due to	wegen
essential	sehr wichtig
estimate	schätzen
execution	Ausführung
expensive	teuer
extremely	äußerst
failure	Mißerfolg, Scheitern
faith; in good ~	in gutem Glauben
from stock	ab Lager
good time; in ~	rechtzeitig
hopefully	hoffentlich
inability	Unfähigkeit
lead to	dazu führen
let down	enttäuschen

loss	Verlust
lost	verloren
overdue	überfällig
pass	vergehen
past	vergangen
point out	betonen
promise	Versprechen
receipt; in ~	im Besitz
reliable	zuverlässig
ship	versenden
shipment	Sendung
shipping agent	Reedereivertreter
stock; in ~	auf Lager
unsatisfactory	nicht zufriedenstellend
urgently	dringend
various	verschieden
virtually	nahezu
what on earth!	Was in aller Welt!

↔ Put it Another Way: Alternative phrases

Starting

the goods ordered by us on 12th June	die von uns am 12. Juni bestellten Waren
our letter of 21st November has not been answered	unser Brief vom 21. November ist nicht beantwortet worden
we are sorry to inform you that ...	es tut uns leid, Ihnen mitteilen zu müssen, daß ...
we are forced to complain about the delay in delivery	wir müssen uns über den Lieferverzug beschweren

Complaining

the delay puts us in a difficult position	der Verzug bringt uns in eine schwierige Lage
an early delivery was guaranteed	eine prompte Lieferung wurde garantiert
complying with the delivery dates is essential	die Einhaltung der Liefertermine ist äußerst wichtig
the delay was more than three weeks	der Verzug betrug mehr als drei Wochen
we must insist that you observe delivery dates for future orders	wir müssen darauf bestehen, daß Sie bei künftigen Bestellungen die Liefertermine beachten

Ending

we will be pleased to have your explanation for the long delay	wir wären für eine Erklärung der langen Verzögerung dankbar
we ask you to look into the matter	wir bitten Sie, die Angelegenheit zu untersuchen
please hasten the delivery	bitte bringen Sie die Lieferung schnell auf den Weg

B Brain Work Thirty Two: A little quiz

Now try and put in the correct word into each sentence. There are three possible words but only one correct word.

a) compelled b) assured c) overdue

1) The firm ... us that the goods would arrive on time.

a) consignment b) reliable c) delay

2) The long ... in the execution of your order is unsatisfactory.

a) cancel b) sign c) lengthen

3) If the goods do not arrive next week we will ... the order.

a) contracted b) stocked c) placed

4) We ... the order last month.

a) executed b) passed c) replied

5) Three weeks have ... but we still do not have the shipment.

B Brain Work Thirty Three: Sort out the letter

Here are parts of a letter complaining about a delay in delivery. Please put them in the best order.

1) That was three weeks ago.
2) We are forced to complain about the delay in our order No D546.
3) We will be compelled to cancel the consignment if the goods do not arrive by next week.
4) You assured us that the goods would be here within a week.
5) The delay puts us in a difficult position as we need the goods urgently.
6) We will be pleased to receive your explanation.

Arranging a Meeting

CONTENTS

Joke Time

"No way![1]" said the boss. "I cannot give you two hours off for lunch. Think man, if I did that I would have to do the same for every person whose wife had just had triplets[2]."

1 Kommt nicht in Frage! 2 Drillinge

Focus: Arranging meetings to develop personal relations

It is very important to make and develop personal relations in business. Although the telephone is useful in communicating, very often a meeting can quickly clear up problems and establish good business contacts. Meetings can be arranged by phone but as always in business, it is always good practice to finalize details in writing. Look at the short letter below:

Dear Mrs Lewis

I would appreciate it very much if I could have the opportunity of meeting you personally so that we can discuss future business. As I hope to be in London from 12th to 15th June I thought that it would be possible to meet then. I shall contact your office by phone on my arrival.
Please let me know if you will be free to see me and what time would be best for you.

Regards
Jack Beam

Dialogue: Talking about style in making arrangements

In the purchasing department Jane Parker (**JP**) is talking to a trainee, Rose Hill (**RH**).

JP: Well, on the phone you can say things like 'Can we meet up on Wednesday?' or 'If it's okay with you, how about Wednesday?'. But when you confirm an arrangement in writing then you need to be a little more formal.

RS: Alright, let's say I phone up and say that I will be in the area and I want to see somebody in sales, to discuss an order. I'll be staying at a hotel. If it's alright with you we can fix up a time on such and such a date. Oh yeah, and let us know if you can make it then, before I leave.

JP: We need to think about this. Let's write a letter and say what you want but in good style.

RS: Of course, there is another thing about letters.

JP: And what is that? You mean it's always good to get things on paper to avoid confusion later, like on the phone?

RS: No, it means that every time I arrange a room for a visitor at the King George Hotel I don't have the macho manager chatting me up!

Drop Them a Line: Arranging a meeting

That's how Rose's letter looks:

Dear Mrs Smith

As I will be in Manchester on Monday and Tuesday of next week I would be very pleased if I could arrange to meet you with a view to discussing a new order.
I will be staying in the Royal Hotel near the city centre. Could you please leave a message at reception informing me when it would be convenient to meet.
I would be grateful if you could get in touch with me prior to my departure to say if you will be in the firm during this time. If we can meet I will bring the information and catalogue detailing the equipment you were interested in.
Hoping that we will be able to meet. I look forward to seeing you then.

Yours sincerely
Miss Hill, purchasing

Vocabulary: To help you understand

although	obwohl
avoid	vermeiden
chat me up	mich anquatschen
convenient time	passende Zeit
departure	Abreise
develop	entwickeln
establish	gründen, bilden
finalize	endgültig festlegen

fix up	arrangieren
get in touch with	sich in Verbindung setzen
grateful	dankbar
make it (can you make it?)	schaffen (schaffen Sie es?)
meet up	treffen
message	Nachricht
on my arrival	bei meiner Ankunft
opportunity	Möglichkeit
practice	Gewohnheit, Verfahrensweise
prior to	vor, bevor
reception	Empfang
relation	Beziehung
useful	nützlich
with a view to	mit der Absicht, etwas zu tun

↔ Put it Another Way: Alternative phrases

To start

I would welcome the opportunity to ...	ich würde die Gelegenheit begrüßen, um ...
I would like to call on you	ich würde Sie gern aufsuchen..

Fixing date and time

would 2 o'clock on Friday be convenient?	würde Ihnen Freitag um 14.00 Uhr passen?
I would be pleased/happy/glad if you would suggest a time and date to ...	ich würde mich freuen, wenn Sie eine Zeit und Datum vorschlagen würden, um ...
... please give me a ring. a message will reach me in the office	bitte rufen Sie mich an. Eine Nachricht wird mich im Büro erreichen
if this time/day does not suit you	falls diese Zeit/dieser Tag Ihnen nicht paßt

please suggest an alternative day	bitte schlagen Sie einen anderen Tag vor
would it be at all possible to arrange another meeting?	wäre es überhaupt möglich, einen anderen Termin zu vereinbaren?

Ending the letter

I look forward to meeting you	ich freue mich, Sie zu treffen
it will be a pleasure to see you again	ich freue mich darauf, Sie wiederzusehen
I will be delighted to meet you	ich freue mich sehr, Sie zu treffen

B Brain Work Thirty Four: What's the English for ...?

Over to you! Please put the English word together with the German word.

1) convenient	obwohl
2) grateful	Ankunft
3) opportunity	passend
4) although	dankbar
5) arrival	vor/bevor
6) prior to	Möglichkeit

B Brain Work Thirty Five: Letter writing

Now your turn to do a little work on a letter. Here is a letter partly in German. Please use the phrases and vocabulary in this chapter to replace the German with English.

Dear Mr Barker

Ich würde die Gelegenheit begrüßen to meet you some time next week. *Würde Ihnen Dienstag um 10.00 passen*? *Falls* this day and time are not convenient *bitte schlagen Sie eine andere Zeit und einen anderen Tag vor.*

Please contact me in the company. If I am out *eine Nachricht wird mich im Büro erreichen.*
Ich freue mich sehr, Sie wieder zu treffen

Yours sincerely
A. Lowe, Sales

Letter Box: Prepositions of time

Prepositions of time can be a little tricky but if you look at the examples below you should not make a mistake.

at 9 o'clock / 6.30 a.m.
at midday / midnight
at Easter / Christmas
at the end of March / the moment
at the weekend(s)

on Friday(s) / Monday(s) etc.
on 12th August / 30th April etc.
on Christmasday / Good Friday (Karfreitag)

in June / December
in 1958 / 1066/2005
in (the) spring / autumn / summer / winter
in the afternoon / the evening / the morning

Note: on Monday afternoon / on Friday morning

B Brain Work Thirty Six: Prepositions of time

Please put in the correct preposition of time in the sentences below. Use the information in the Letter Box to help you. Good luck!

1) We will make the delivery ... August.
2) I sent you a fax ... Tuesday afternoon last week.
3) We shall meet you at the airport ... 12 o'clock.
4) The company was established ... 1885 by my great great grandfather.
5) The sales manager will visit your firm some time ... late summer.
6) Our firm does not work ... Wednesday afternoon.
7) We do not work ... the weekends.

More on Meetings

CONTENTS

Focus: Answering invitations to a meeting
Dialogue: Bob Onion expects a visit from Russia
Drop Them a Line: The reply to the Russians
Put It Another Way: Alternative phrases
Brain Work: What's the English for …? plus a little more

Joke Time

Bob Onion called in one of his salesmen[1].
"Sidebottom, you dress well[2], even smartly[3], you are charming in the office and very friendly."
"Well, thank you, sir. I do my best for the firm" said Sidebottom slightly surprised[4] and now expecting a raise.
"That's okay. I was just trying to put you in a good mood[5] before we start to discuss the fact that you are often late, have days off work when you feel like it and have the lowest sales performance[6] in the office."

1 Verkäufer 2 gut angezogen 3 schick 4 etwas überrascht 5 gute Laune 6 niedrigster Umsatz

Focus: Answering invitations to a meeting

If invited to meet a customer either by letter or phone a written response in the form of a letter is very important. This can avoid misunderstandings that at times happen when arrangements are made only on the phone. It is also an opportunity to build up business relationships and good will. Take a look at the letter below.

Dear Mr Nixon

Thank you for your letter dated 21st June of this year informing us that your chief overseas buyer, Mrs McCartney, will be coming to Europe in August. I shall be delighted to meet her then with a view to discussing a number of projects. Please contact me nearer her planned date of arrival. If Mrs McCartney wishes we will be happy to meet her at the airport and arrange accommodation for the duration of her stay.
I very much look forward to meeting Mrs McCartney

Yours sincerely
L. Bronstein

Dialogue: Bob Onion expects a visit from Russia

Bob Onion (**BO**) is talking to his new sales manager, Fiona Merryweather (**FM**). He has just received a letter from the Russian engineering company, Popov Engineering International.

BO: You must listen to this letter!
(*Bob Onion reads the letter*)

Dear Mr Onion
A group of our representatives will be in England next month. We would be glad to visit you in your company with a view to developing business relations.
Mr Podgorny, who visited you last year, will also be there. We will be in Birmingham on 14th to the 17th August and we hope that you will be able to meet our representatives then. Please contact us with your comments. We look forward to hearing from you shortly.

Yours sincerely
A. Popov

FM: Isn't that nice, keeping contact and so on?
BO: This is dreadful news. This Podgorny chap was here last year.
FM: Yes, but didn't you make a deal worth £15,000?
BO: Absolutely right.They are acting as our agents now. We also had to put him in a hotel for weekend then pay the bill.
FM: Well, that's nothing in comparison.
BO: Oh no? There were one or two extras.
FM: That's normal too!
BO: While he was here I had to accompany him virtually everywhere he went. I had a hangover for five days and this time a group of them are coming! No, write and tell them I'm on holiday, in hospital, in prison or gone to become a monk in a monastry. You and your colleagues can deal with it. That's what you are paid for.
FM: Mmm! Mr Abdul Azis from Saudi will be here, too. Maybe Mr Podgorny could show him round.
BO: I do hope that you are pulling my leg. I don't think they will have a lot in common apart from buying our products, I hope. Oh, and another thing, last year it was just Popov Ltd.
FM: Well?
BO: Now they are Popov International. Lord help us!

Drop Them a Line: The reply to the Russians

Following the conversation between Onion and Merryweather, Popov gets a letter from Onions:

Dear Mr Popov

It is with considerable regret that I have to advise you that Mr Onion will be away for the first two weeks of August. However, myself and other members of the sales department will be pleased to welcome you.
Please get in touch with us as soon as you arrive in England.
Yours sincerely

Fiona Merryweather
Sales Manager

Ⓥ Vocabulary: To help you understand

able to do; be ~	etwas können
accommodation	Unterkunft
accompany	begleiten
advise	informieren/mitteilen
arrival	Ankunft
avoid	vermeiden
chap	Kerl
charming	charmant
chief	Haupt-
common	gemeinsam
comparison	Vergleich
considerable; with ~ regret	mit großem Bedauern
day off	Tag frei
delighted	entzückt
dreadful	schrecklich
duration	Dauer
glad	froh
good mood	gute Laune
good will	Wohlwollen
hangover	Kater
invite	einladen
invitation	Einladung
member	Mitglied
monk	Mönch
opportunity	Möglichkeit
overseas	Übersee
performance	Leistung
pull somebody's leg	jemanden auf den Arm nehmen
regret	Bedauern
representative	Vertreter
response	Antwort
right	richtig
shortly	bald

slightly	etwas, ein kleines bißchen
smart	schick
stay	Aufenthalt
virtually	fast
with a view to	mit der Absicht, etwas zu tun

↔ Put It Another Way: Alternative phrases

unfortunately the manager is in Japan at the moment	leider ist der Manager zur Zeit in Japan
I am afraid that I must cancel the meeting with the export manager	leider muß ich die Besprechung mit dem Exportleiter absagen
I am sorry that I had call you to postpone the meeting	es tut mir leid, daß ich Sie anrufen mußte, um die Zusammenkunft zu verschieben
I expect to be back in the office on Tuesday	ich nehme an, daß ich am Dienstag wieder im Büro sein werde
would it be convenient for you to meet me for lunch?	wäre es Ihnen recht, wenn wir uns zum Mittagessen treffen?
thank you for your kind invitation	danke für Ihre freundliche Einladung
it is most kind of you to invite me to dinner on Wednesday	es ist äußerst freundlich von Ihnen, mich am Mittwoch zum Mittagessen einzuladen
it will be good to see you again	ich freue mich, Sie wiederzusehen
I cannot accept your invitation owing to a previous engagement	ich kann Ihre Einladung wegen einer früheren Verpflichtung nicht annehmen

(B) Brain Work Thirty Seven: What's the English for...?

To test your memory put the English and German words together.

1) postpone	a) bedauern
2) convenient	b) verschieben
3) cancel	c) Einladung
4) at the moment	d) passend
5) regret	e) absagen
6) invitation	f) augenblicklich

(B) Brain Work Thirty Eight: Complete the sentences

Please put in the words below into the sentences and check the meaning with the words in this chapter.

expect kind owing afraid unfortunately convenient

1) ... I cannot meet you for dinner tomorrow.
2) Would it be ... to meet you in two weeks?
3) I want to thank you for your ... invitation.
4) ... to a previous engagement I cannot see you next Monday.
5) I am...that I must postpone the meeting.
6) I ... to be in London on 19th May.

(B) Brain Work Thirty Nine: Let's look at a few words

Here are some words from this chapter with letters missing. Please complete the word and give the German for it.

1) in-i-ati-n	means	....	in German
2) -pp-rt-n-ty		....	
3) r-sp-n-e		....	
4) ov-rs—s		....	
5) -cco-mod-t-on		....	
6) p-rform-n-e		....	

Chapter 14

Complaints

CONTENTS

Focus: Complaining customer
Dialogue: Onions receive the wrong order
Drop Them a Line: Onions complain and get a reply.
Other complaints.
Put It Another Way: Alternative phrases
Brain Work: Complete a letter and solve a quiz

Joke Time

The boss: Good grief, this letter is full of mistakes. The punctuation[1] is dreadful[2] and the spelling is lousy[3]! Didn't you check it to see if it was okay?
The secretary: I would have but didn't you say that the letter was strictly private and confidential[4]?

1 Zeichensetzung 2 schrecklich 3 lausig 4 streng vertraulich

Focus: Complaining customer

A customer may complain about a number of different things. The goods may be defective or spoilt in some way. They may have been damaged during transport.
The goods received by the customer may not correspond to type, quality or quantity ordered. If the seller fails to deliver as agreed the goods will be placed at his/her disposal. Any payment made by the buyer should be refunded. If the buyer still wants to have the goods he/she does not annul the contract but rather asks for replacements. To promote goodwill the seller should always be ready to admit an error. Often, seller and buyer will reach compromises. Only in the worst cases do firms settle difficulties by going to law. This costs a lot of money and wastes time.

Dialogue: Onions receive the wrong order

One Monday, Robin Hodgeson (**RH**), manager of the store of Onions, comes into the purchasing department to talk to Ian Miller (**IM**), one of the buyers.

RH: We had a delivery last week of copper pipes from Tyzacks and I think you should know that there are a few problems.
IM: Really? What problems?
RH: When we opened the crate we saw they had sent 150 T-joints instead of 300 bends. They also sent us 400 plastic brackets.
IM: We didn't order any brackets, plastic or metal.
RH: What do you want me to do with them?
IM: I'll drop them a line and ask them what's going on.
RH: Okay, but in the meantime we need the bends. What do you think?
IM: Bends? I'll just have to see what Tyzacks say. Maybe they can send us the bends straight away by special delivery.
IM: Well, sorry about the joke but the engineers are complaining about not having bends and it's driving me right round the bend!
IM: Very funny, but I've heard that joke before in this company.

Drop Them a Line: Onions complain and get a reply

Here is the letter Ian wrote to Tyzacks:

For the attention of the Sales Department

Dear Sirs

I regret that I must call your attention to the last order you sent us, order no P460, which arrived on 13th June. Although most of the order was correct, you have sent us a box of 150 T-joints marked F104 instead of the 300 bends we actually ordered. In addition the crate contained 400 plastic brackets which we did not order.
Although we may need the T-joints in the future we have no requirement for brackets. As well as this we need the 300 bends urgently.
Please let us have your comments with regard to this matter.

Yours faithfully
Ian Miller

With good business practice, a company should always reply to a complaint. Here is the reply from Tyzacks to Onions:

Dear Mr Miller

Thank you for your letter dated 16th June concerning order no P460.
I am both surprised and sorry to hear about the problems with the make up of the order. I am sure you will agree that we are a regular and reliable supplier and this is the first time that such an error has occurred. I will despatch a box of 300 bends to you immediately by special delivery.
As far as the brackets are concerned I shall arrange to pick them up next week. Please inform me if you wish to keep the T-joints. I am willing to grant a 10% discount on this item for causing you inconvenience.

Yours sincerely
Barry Noble

Here are some other complaints

Citroflip, a tropical fruit distribtor and wholesaler, writes to a supplier:

Dear Sirs

We were most disappointed with the latest delivery of mixed fruit.
The bananas were overripe and could not be sold and half the oranges had clearly been badly bruised while being shipped.
In addition, we found, upon weighing the dried dates that every bag was two or three pounds underweight.
We trust you will look into this matter and let us know as soon as possible what action you intend to take.

Yours faithfully

A department store writes to a clothing supplier:

Dear Sirs

We are sorry to report that upon careful inspection of your recent consignment of woollen socks we found that the quality did not correspond to that of the samples you originally sent us.
When placing the order we stressed the importance of high quality as our customers are accustomed to only the best.
We can only assume that this is an oversight on your part. If not, and you are unable to supply us, we will be forced to terminate the contract and take our custom elsewhere.
We must ask you to take prompt action as we cannot sell these socks and there is great demand for such items due to the present cold weather.
We await your reply with interest.

Yours faithfully

Vocabulary: To help you understand

accustomed to	gewöhnt daran
actually	eigentlich, in der Tat
addition; in ~	außerdem
admit	zugeben

agreed; as ~	vereinbaren (wie vereinbart)
annul	annullieren
as far as ... is concerned	was ... betrifft
assure	versichern
attention; for the ~ of ...	zu Händen von ....
badly bruised (fruit)	(Obst) mit schlimmen Druckstellen
bend	Bogen
box	Karton
bracket	Anschluß
case	Fall
cause	verursachen
clothing	Kleidung
complain	beklagen, Beschwerde einlegen
complaint	Beschwerde
confidential	vertraulich
contain	enthalten
copper pipe	Kupferrohr
correspond	entsprechen
crate	Kiste
custom	Kundschaft
damaged	beschädigt
defective	fehlerhaft, defekt
demand	Nachfrage
disappointed	enttäuscht
discount	Rabatt
disposal; placed at the ~	zur Verfügung gestellt
dried dates	getrocknete Datteln
drive me round the bend	mich verrückt machen
elsewhere	anderswo
error	Fehler
fail to do	etwas nicht tun, etwas unterlassen
force	zwingen
going on (what is going on?)	was ist los?
grant	gewähren
importance	Wichtigkeit

inconvenience	Unbequemlichkeit, Unannehmlichkeit
inspection	Kontrolle
instead of	anstelle
intend	beabsichtigen
item	Artikel
law; go to ~	vor Gericht gehen
let somebody have something	jemandem etwas schicken
look into	prüfen
make up	Zusammensetzung
matter	Angelegenheit
occur	passieren
overripe	überreif
oversight	Versehen
pick up	abholen
promote	fördern
punctuation	Zeichensetzung
recent	neulich
refund	zurückzahlen
regular	regelmäßig
reliable	zuverlässig
replacement	Ersatz
report	berichten
requirement	Bedürfnis
sample	Muster
settle	erledigen, klären
special delivery	Sonderlieferung
spelling	Rechtschreibung
spoilt	verdorben
store	Lager
stress	betonen
strictly	streng
surprised	überrascht
T-joint	T-Stück
take action	etwas unternehmen
terminate	lösen

to call attention to	auf etwas aufmerksam machen
upon; ~ opening	bei (beim Öffnen)
unable	unfähig
underweight	untergewichtig
waste	verschwenden
weigh	wiegen
wholesaler	Großhändler
with regard to	hinsichtlich

Put it Another Way: Alternative phrases

Starting the letter

we are forced to notify you ...	wir müssen Ihnen leider mitteilen
we are sorry that we must complain about ...	leider müssen wir ... reklamieren.
we feel forced to point out that ...	wir müssen darauf hinweisen, daß ...

Complaints

crate no. 2 contains articles which we did not order	Kiste Nr. 2 enthält Artikel, die wir nicht bestellt haben
on/upon opening the box we found that it contained ...	beim Öffnen der Kiste stellten wir fest, daß ...
we cannot possibly accept these products as/because ...	wir können diese Waren unmöglich akzeptieren, da ...
it is clear that a mistake has been made	offensichtlich wurde ein Fehler gemacht
the goods were badly damaged when delivered	die Waren waren bei der Anlieferung schwer beschädigt

Ending the letter

we must insist that ...	wir müssen darauf bestehen, daß ...
we look forward to your reply	wir erwarten Ihre Antwort
we hope that this error will not occur again	wir hoffen, daß ein solcher Fehler nicht wieder vorkommt

B Brain Work Forty: Complete the letter

Over to you! Please put in the words below into the gaps in the letter.

inconvenience instead mistake point out as soon as upon

Dear Sirs

We are sorry to ... (1) ... that ... (2) ... opening crate no.7 we found that a ... (3) ... had been made ... (4) ... of the twenty 10 kilo bags of Darjeling tea, first quality, we received twenty 5 kilo bags.
This has caused us some ... (5) ...
Please let us have 100 extra kilos of the tea ... (6) .... possible.

Yours faithfully

B Brain Work Forty One: Quiz time

Please tick the correct answer and test your memory.

1) A customer may complain if:

a) the goods are damaged
b) bills are paid
c) the seller is polite

2) "To reach a compromise" means here

a) seller and buyer go to law
b) seller and buyer make a deal
c) the seller makes an error

3) If a seller refunds a buyer:

a) the buyer gets money back
b) the buyer gets replacements
c) the seller says sorry

4) "I annulled the contract" This means:

a) I lost the contract
b) I cancelled the contract
c) I wrote "0"on the contract

5) "The goods do not correspond to the quality ordered" means

a) the products are not good enough
b) the products are delayed
c) the products are spoilt

6) If the seller sends the wrong quality the seller should:

a) never admit the error
b) admit the error
c) invite the customer for lunch

Credit Matters

CONTENTS

Joke Time

Employee: Can I have the day off[1] tomorrow to go Christmas shopping with my wife?
Boss: You certainly can't, we are far too busy.
Employee: Thank's a lot.

1 den Tag frei haben

Focus: Credit enquiries

In business it is normal for customers to ask for credit. The supplier must find out if the customer is creditworthy, especially if the supplier has not done business with the customer before. There are different ways to get information on a customer. A customer can supply trade references. This means that the customer gives the names of previous companies with whom business has been done. An alternative is that the customer gives the name of his or her bank. The customer can also provide information in the form recent balance sheets proving the solvency of his or her company. There are also so-called credit-enquiry agencies which can investigate a company's creditworthiness.
When someone writes to a firm asking for credit information this is confidential.
The letter may not have the name of the firm on it but the name of the firm is written on a separate slip of paper attatched to the letter.
Reports on companies are usually cautious bcause of laws on libel and slander. If a firm does not give a report on a firm this is almost the same as giving a bad report.

Dialogue: How to put an enquiry about credit

Terry Jones (**TJ**) at Onions has been given the job of writing a letter to another firm to enquire about the creditworthiness of another company. Here he is talking to one of the secretaries, Helen Stevens (**HS**).

TJ: You know, I've got no idea at all about this. I mean I understand why we need to know if a firm can pay their bills on time but when I asked the boss about this he said that I should be 'cautious' about what I said and something about 'slander and libel law'.

HS: So what did you say then?

TJ: I'll read you what I wrote. 'Dear Sir, your name was given us by Stockman and Son. You have done business with them before, they said. Please ...' the boss said I should be polite as this is asking a favour. Where was I? Oh yes 'Please tell us if they are solvent and if they pay on time. We are thinking about doing £10,000 of business with them. Thank you for your cooperation in this matter and we will treat the information confidentially' The last bit was the boss's idea, you know 'cooperation in this matter' and 'treat the blah, blah confidentially'. What do you think?

HS: Not bad apart from the fact that you shouldn't give the name in the letter.

TJ: What? How do they know who I'm talking about? I mean ...

HS: Hold on, hold on! You should write the name on a slip of paper and enclose it in the envelope. And the style could be better.

TJ: Okay, are you busy at the moment? Can you give me a few tips?

Drop Them a Line: Onions ask for information

Here is the letter that Helen and Terry wrote:

Dear Sirs

Your name has been given to us by the firm mentioned on the slip attached.
Would you please give us information with regard to the standing of the company and their reliability. Do you consider it safe to grant a credit of about £10,000?
We thank you very much for your cooperation and any information provided will be treated in the strictest confidence.

Yours faithfully

Vocabulary: To help you understand

apart from	abgesehen von
balance sheet	Bilanz
cautious	vorsichtig
certainly not	sicher nicht
confidential	vertraulich
consider	denken
credit enquiry agency	Kreditauskunftei

creditworthiness	Kreditwürdigkeit
hold on!	Moment mal!
investigate	überprüfen
law	Gesetz
libel	Verleumdung
mention	erwähnen
previous	vorherig, vorhergehend
prove	beweisen
provide	liefern
recent	neulich
report	Bericht, berichten
slander	Beleidigung
slip of paper	Blatt Papier
solvency	Zahlungsfähigkeit
standing	Ruf
strictest	strengst
trade references	Handelsreferenz
treat	behandeln
with regard to	in bezug auf

↔ Put It Another Way: Alternative phrases

please let us have information about the firm	bitte geben Sie uns Auskünfte über die Firma
you were named as a reference	Sie wurden als Referenz genannt
as we have never done business with this firm before	da wir nie Geschäfte mit dieser Firma gemacht haben
as this firm is unknown to us	da wir diese Firma nicht kennen
please provide us with the usual trade reference	bitte geben Sie die üblichen Handelsreferenzen an
is the firm reliable and sound?	ist die Firma zuverlässig und solid?

we will treat the information with discretion	wir werden die Auskunft mit Verschwiegenheit behandeln
we hope we can be of assistance to you in a similar case	wir hoffen, daß wir Ihnen in einem ähnlichen Fall helfen können

B Brain Work Forty Two: Complete the letter

Please put in the words below into the letter and see what you can remember.

assistance	consider	reference	information
slip	reliable	discretion	grant

Dear Sirs

Private and Confidential
You have been named as a ... (1) ... by the firm mentioned on the ... (2) ... attached.
Please let us have ... (3) ... about the firm as we have never done business with them before. Is the firm ... (4) ... and sound? Do you ... (5) ... it safe to ... (6) ... a credit of about £12,000?
The information will be treated with ... (7) ...
We hope we can be of ... (8) ... in a similar case in future.

Yours faithfully

B Brain Work Forty Three: Words from the chapter

Here are some words from the chapter with letters missing. Please put in the missing letters and give the German for the word.

1) p-evi-us means in German ....?
2) st-n-ing ....?
3) r-cent ....?
4) -olve-cy ....?
5) con-id-nt-a- ....?
6) cr-dit-ort-y ....?

B Brain Work Forty Four: Quiz time

Over to you to see what you remember from 'Focus on credit enquiries'. Here are some questions about credit letters. Please say if they are true or false.

1) It is important for a company to be creditworthy. T / F
2) It is not possible for a customer to prove her/ his creditworthiness. T / F
3) A credit-enquiry agency investigates the quality of goods. T / F
4) When you write to a firm asking about the creditworthyness of another company you should write the name, address and phone number of the firm clearly at the top of the page. T / F
5) A libel is a sort of bill. T / F
6) Solvent means that you can pay. T / F

Letter Box: When to use "date" and "appointment"

Date and appointment are two words that can cause confusion.

Date means Termin and Verabredung but also has the meaning of Rendezvous.

Appointment is more official. Normally it means a less official meeting.

For example "I have a date with my boyfriend."
Sometimes it is used loosely to mean something more official.
For example "Please arrange a date with the manager."

If it was clearly business you would use appointment.
You would not say "I have a date with the doctor."

Of course if the doctor was your boy or girlfriend then you could say date.

Look at this joke as an example

Sales representative: "I've been trying to see you for a week. Can we arrange to see each other some time next week?"
Boss of firm: "Please arrange a date with Miss Noden, my secretary."
Sales representative: "Well, I did and we had a very good time but I still need to see you to discuss business".

Chapter 16

Fairs and Exhibitions

CONTENTS

Focus: The role of trade fairs
Dialogue: Onions discuss participation at a trade fair
Drop Them a Line: Onions ask about a trade fair in Frankfurt
Put It Another Way: Alternative phrases
Brain Work: Memory test, completing a letter and a quiz

Joke Time

Bob Onion: So Gerry, did you decide[1] anything important at the conference in Bermuda last week?
Salesman: Actually yes. We decided[1] to have another conference there next month.

Two representatives[2] on the way to a trade fair in Bradford are talking on the train.
First rep: Have you been to the fair very often? It's my first visit.
Second: Actually[3] I've been here every year since 1986.
First: And what hotel would you recommend?[4] I hope I can still get a room.
Second: Try the Station Hotel.
First: Oh, have you stayed there before?
Second: No, never, but I've stayed in all the others.

1 beschließen 2 Vertreter 3 eigentlich 4 empfehlen

Focus: The role of trade fairs and exhibitions

Trade fairs and exhibitions are very important for passing on information and ideas. Normally they are only for business people and a lot of business is generated at fairs. Fairs and exhibitions specialize in one area or they may have a variety of products on display.

Dialogue: Onions discuss participation at a trade fair

Bob Onion (**BO**), the boss, Ian Miller (**IM**) and Gerry Murry (**GM**) from sales are planning taking part at a trade fair for heating equipment and other engineering products in Frankfurt.

BO: This will cost a lot of money but we need to try to get ourselves a name on the continent.
IM: And at the same time see what the competition is doing over there.
BO: You two need to go and take two engineers.
GM: And what about a secretary?
BO: Four people will be expensive enough with hotel costs, cost of a stand or booth. What do you need your secretary for?
GM: In case I need to write letters and somebody to take short hand.
BO: Total rubbish! You can leave the letter writing until you come back.
GM: Ah, well, Miss Brahms speaks very good German and we are all hopeless at foreign languages.
BO: Luckily one of the new engineers who is coming with you speaks German.
GM: I suppose he's some big hairy rugby type.
BO: Actually, he's a she. In fact both engineers are 'shes'.
GM: Oh well, that's different.
BO: Really. Well I want you to write a letter to reserve a good spot in the hall.

Drop Them a Line: Onions ask about a trade fair in Frankfurt

Now take a look at the letter sent by Onions to the organisers of Heating 1997 Trade Fair:

Dear Sirs

We have had our attention drawn to your trade fair in Frankfurt, dates 14th to 20th October of this coming year.
Our firm, based in Birmingham in UK, develops and produces equipment for the heating engineering industry.
As we wish to make contact with customers in Europe, participation at your trade fair would be an ideal opportunity for us to meet people in our field in Germany.
Could you please forward us details including information about the cost of renting exhibition space and the conditions for taking part.

Your faithfully
Ian Miller

Vocabulary: To help you understand

attention (draw attention to something)	Aufmerksamkeit (auf etwas lenken)
booth	Stand
competition	Konkurrenz
Continent	Kontinentaleuropa
dates ... to ...	vom ... bis zum ...
display (on display)	Ausstellung (ausgestellt sein)
equipment	Ausrüstung
exhibition	Ausstellung
foreign language	Fremdsprache
forward	senden
generate (be generated)	entstehen
get a name	bekannt werden
hairy	haarig
hopeless	hoffnungslos

including	einschließlich
opportunity	Möglichkeit
participate	teilnehmen
participation	Teilnahme
rent	mieten
shorthand	Kurzschrift
spot	Stelle
stand	Stand
suppose	annehmen, vermuten
take part	teilnehmen
toy	Spielzeug
trade fair	Handelsmesse
variety	Vielfalt, Auswahl

↔ To Put It Another Way: Alternative phrases

we wish to exhibit our goods at the fair	wir möchten unsere Waren auf der Messe ausstellen
we wish to organize/stage an exhibition	wir möchten eine Ausstellung veranstalten
is it still possible to rent/book exhibition space?	ist es noch möglich, Ausstellungsfläche zu mieten?
I wish to apply for space at a fair	ich möchte mich um Ausstellungsfläche bewerben
when is the deadline for applications?	wann ist Anmeldeschluß?
will the fees be refunded?	werden die Gebühren zurückerstattet?
we wish to cancel/withdraw our application	wir möchten unsere Anmeldung zurückziehen
when can we put up our stand?	wann können wir unseren Stand aufstellen?
when must we remove/dismantle our stand?	wann müssen wir unseren Stand abbauen?

our catalogues will be available to the visiting buyers	unsere Kataloge werden dem Käuferpublikum zur Verfügung stehen

B Brain Work Forty Five: Test your memory

And now put together the English and German words.

1) exhibition	a) Möglichkeit
2) participate	b) Handelsmesse
3) including	c) Ausstellung
4) variety	d) einschließlich
5) opportunity	e) Vielfalt/Auswahl
6) trade fair	f) teilnehmen

B Brain Work Forty Six: Complete the letter

Please complete the letter below using the phrases and words from this chapter. Here are the words to help you. Good luck!

a) forward	b) attention	c) exhibited	d) cancel
e) space	f) staged	g) deadline	h) fees

Dear Sirs

Last week our ... (1) ... was drawn to the trade fair, International Games and Toys Fair 19.. , which will be ... (2) ... by you in Dublin.
We are producers of high quality mechanical and electrical toys with our main factory near York.
As this is the first time we have ... (3) ... our goods at your fair we would like some information.
When is the ... (4) ... for applications? We hope that we are not too late and it is still possible to rent exhibition ... (5) ...?
If we wish to ... (6) ... our application will all the ... (7) ... be refunded?
Could you please ... (8) ... details including the cost of a small stand for 4 days?

Your faithfully

B Brain Work Forty Seven: Quiz time

Last but not least a small quiz on the chapter.

1) Trade fairs are normally for:

a) business people only
b) all people
c) engineers

2) "Stage a fair" means:

a) cancel a fair
b) organize a fair
c) rent space at a fair

3) The German for "participate" is:

a) ausstellen
b) annehmen
c) teilnehmen

4) At a trade fair I would expect to see:

a) stands
b) check-in desks
c) a football match

5) Which is correct?

a) My attention was drawn to ...
b) My attention was pulled to ...
c) My attention was linked to ...

6) A "deadline" is:

a) A time after which a person dies
b) A train line that is not used
c) A last possible date or time

Chapter 17

Banking

CONTENTS

Focus: Banks and banking
Dialogue: At Greyfellows Bank
Drop Them a Line: Letters about overdrafts
Put It Another Way: Alternative phrases
Brain Work: Complete a letter and make a memory test

Joke Time

My uncle who had overdrawn[1] his account[2] by too much received a sarcastic[3] letter from his bank manager.

Dear Mr Hemming

I have noticed that your account is now overdrawn well over the limit[4] and has been for some time. Can we please return to the original arrangement where you bank with us and not we bank with you?

Yours sincerely

The son of a business man was asked at school by the teacher:
"If your father borrowed[5] £50,000 from his bank and agreed to pay £5,000 of the loan[6] back every month, how much would he have paid after eight months?"
"£5,000."
"You don't know much about mathematics, Barry, do you?"
"And you don't know much about my father."

1 überzogen 2 Konto 3 sarkastisch 4 weit über das Limit 5 borgen 6 Darlehen

Focus: Banks and Banking

Banking performs a number of vital services both for the general public and business. For most people banks accept deposits, in other words you pay in money and the bank keeps it. The two main types of account are savings account and current account. The savings account is for people who want to save money and have an account that pays them a higher rate of interest. However, the money cannot be taken out or withdrawn as easily as with a current account. Almost all people and all businesses have a current account. It is very flexible as money is always at the customer's disposal. Bills can be paid by cheque, transfer, direct debit and standing order. More importantly the customer can borrow money. This credit can be a loan or overdraft. The bank will usually require some type of security for this. Banks are also important for helping to advise customers on the creditworthiness of firms, and paying bills from other countries and helping with various aspects of foreign trade.

Dialogue: At Greyfellows Bank

Greyfellows is a nation-wide bank in Britain. It is Onions' bank. Well, Onions do not own it but banks there. Here Miss Babcock (**B**) from the lending department is talking to Mr Stuffy (**S**), the manager:

B: Well, Mr Stuffy, I must say that I think we should contact Onion about the level of his overdraft. His facility is £700 per month but he is £1500 in the red.

S: Is that young Onion or old Onion?

B: I'm afraid it's young Onion, and we have already written to him threatening to withdraw his credit facility.

S: Miss Babcock! You can't possibly threaten our customers, especially an old trusted and reliable firm like Onions, and especially as I know old Mr Onion personally. I was at school with him you know ..., or was it his father? Whatever, we don't threaten, oh no! We advise our customers.

B: Still, I do think we must take some action. I'll send a firm letter asking when he intends to get his overdraft in order. Unless you want to talk to his father personally at the golf course that is?

S: Ehr, pardon? I'll ignore that remark, Miss Babcock. Whatever you young types think, the old personal contact is still important.
B: I'll write a really firm letter then.

Drop Them a Line: Letters about overdraft

Greyfellows bank sends a letter to young Onion:

21st February 19..
Dear Mr Onion

It has come to our attention that your account is overdrawn by £1,704.54 pence.
This is despite the fact that your originally agreed facility was well under half that, £700 to be precise. It is also despite the fact that we wrote to you on two previous occasions, 12th December 19.. and 24th January 19.., asking you to explain the reason for the delay in putting your account in the black.
Since then we have heard nothing. In fact the account was further overdrawn. If we do not hear from you within seven days we are forced to advise you that your credit facility will be suspended, and your account frozen.
We regret having to take this action but the lack of response means that we have no choice.

Yours sincerely

Miss Tracy Babcock
Lending Department

Barry Onion writes back:

Dear Miss Babcock

It was with great surprise that I received you letter of 21st February 19.. .
The delay in my replying to your letters before is that I was very ill with a tropical disease in the small African country, Twinanda, where I was doing voluntary work for a well-known charity.

You may wonder why the account was overdrawn due to a cheque paying £1305 to a travel agent Short's Caribbean Cruisers Ltd. when I was in Africa. The answer is simply that it was a poor relative's birthday, my old aunty Mavis, so I paid for her holiday.
You may also notice £206 withdrawn from my account direct debit at Guppy's Diving Equipment Shop. This is due to my aunty being a keen swimmer even though she is eighty five.
The overdraft will be cleared within the next few days from my father's account.

Yours sincerely
Barry Onion

Ⓥ Vocabulary: To help you understand

account	Konto
advise	verständigen, unterrichten, beraten
attention; it has come to our ~	wir sind darauf aufmerksam geworden
banking	Bankwesen
charity	Wohltätigkeitsverein
clear	begleichen
credit facility	Kreditrahmen
current account	laufendes Konto
deposit	deponieren, Einlage, Guthaben
despite the fact that	trotz der Tatsache, daß
direct debit	Einzugsermächtigung
disposal; at my disposal ~	Verfügung; zu meiner ~
diving equipment	Tauchgeräte
facility	Einrichtung, Möglichkeit
firm	streng; bestimmt
frozen	blockiert

general public	Publikum, Öffentlichkeit
intend	beabsichtigen
interest (rate of interest)	Zinsen (Zinssatz)
in the black	in den schwarzen Zahlen
in the red	in den roten Zahlen
keen on	stark interessiert an
lending department	Kreditabteilung
level	Ebene
loan	Darlehen
occasion	Mal, Gelegenheit
overdraft	Überziehung
overdraw	überziehen
perform	leisten, durchführen
precise	genau
previous	vorherig
rate	Satz, Kurs
relative	Verwandte
remark	Bemerkung
require	benötigen; erfordern
savings account	Sparkonto
security	Sicherheit
service	Dienstleistung
standing order	Dauerauftrag
surprise	überraschen
suspend an account	sperren; ein Konto ~
take action	Schritte unternehmen
threaten	drohen
transfer	überweisen
tropical disease	tropische Krankheit
trusted	vertrauenswürdig
vital	lebenswichtig
voluntary work	freiwillige Arbeit
whatever	wie auch immer
withdraw	abheben

↔ Put It Another Way: Alternative phrases

please open/close account No ...	bitte eröffnen/auflösen Konto Nr. ...
we would be pleased if you would arrange a credit of ...	wir wären dankbar, wenn Sie uns einen Kredit von ... gewähren würden
please allow us a loan of £20,000 for a period of 6 months	gewähren Sie uns bitte ein Darlehen von £20,000 für die Zeit von 6 Monaten
we need a loan as ...	wir brauchen ein Darlehen, weil ...
as security we wish to offer you	als Sicherheit können wir Ihnen bieten
I would be ready to call at the bank and discuss the matter	ich wäre gern bereit, Sie in der Bank aufzusuchen, um die Sache zu besprechen

B Brain Work Forty Eight: Complete the letter

Over to you! Please complete the following letter asking for a loan by replacing the German words with English ones.

Dear Sir

We are writing to ask *Sie uns ein Darlehen von £20,000 für 12 Monate zu gewähren.*
Wir brauchen das Darlehen to buy new machines for our factory. We are sure that as *Kunden* of many years you will agree we are a creditworthy company.
Als Sicherheit können wir Ihnen bieten share certificates worth £25,000.
If you wish to discuss the *Sache, wäre ich gern bereit* to visit you *in der Bank.*

Yours faithfully

B Brain Work Forty Nine: Memory test

Take a try at completing these words from the chapter and then give the German word.

1) ov-rdr-f-	means in German	............?
2) ac-o-nt		............?
3) cu-r-nt acc-un-		............?
4) t-ansf-r		............?
5) l-an		............?
6) ch-q-e		............?

18 Chapter

Applying for a Job

CONTENTS

Focus: Job application types
Dialogue: In the personnel department
Drop Them a Line: A curriculum vitae and two covering letters
Put It Another Way: Alternative phrases
Brain Work: Correct the spelling mistakes, and a little translation work

Joke Time

The boss of the accounts[1] department at Onions, Barry White, was interviewing a young woman for the post as his private secretary.
To show him that she was intelligent and a quick thinker she said:
"One of my main interests is doing really difficult crossword puzzles[2]. I have even won prizes".
"Really, that's most interesting," said White, "but you see I'm looking for someone who is intelligent and on the ball[3] during office hours."
"Oh," said the candidate, "but that was in office hours!"

1 Buchführung 2 Kreuzworträtsel 3 auf Zack sein

Focus: Job application types

There are two types of written job application. The first is the solicited application. This is a letter in response to an advertisement in the press found in the section called 'situations vacant'. The second type is called the unsolicited application. Such applications are sent on the chance of a vacancy, often on the advice of a friend. Some people would call this 'applying on spec'.

A very important part of the application is the CV or curriculum vitae. This has all the details about the applicant including education, training and relevant experience. Sometimes copies of certificates must be submitted. Some firms and organisations ask applicants to fill in or complete special application forms.

Dialogue: In the personnel department

In Onions, Sue Onion (**SO**), the boss's daughter, has started work in the personnel department. Here she is talking to Judy James (**JJ**), the head of the department, about today's work.

JJ: Well, Sue, today we are going to look at those applications for the job we advertised in last Friday's 'Birmingham Globe'. The first thing to do is take a look at the curriculum vitae to see if the applicants have the minimum qualifications, then we'll weed out the untidy ones with spelling mistakes in the covering letter.

SO: So, I'll look at the, er cur ..., cura vita ..., curious vitals, and check on the exams the applicants passed?

JJ: Curriculum vitae! Curriculum vitae!

SO: Sorry, I was never very good at French. Anyway, the CV.

JJ: Yes, and then take a look at the letters. Think about your own application and how you would write it. You know that the application is the first impression that we get so presentation is as important as the candidate's qualifications.

SO: Could I take a look at a CV and some letters and you tell me what is good and what isn't so good? You see I didn't write a covering letter.

JJ: You mean you filled in an application form?

SO: Well, my dad filled it in for me and only my name and address.

JJ: I see. Well, take a look at this good CV and two letters. One is too informal and the other is okay. You tell me which is best.

Drop Them a Line: A curriculum vitae and two covering letters

Curriculum vitae

Name:	Julius Eric Cheeser	
Address:	16 Beechhill Road, Sheffield, Yorkshire, S10 2SB	
Telephone:	(0742) 683375	
Date of Birth:	11th July, 1965	
Education:		
1972 to 1983	King Edward's High School GCE "O" Level 8 passes "A" Level 3 passes	
Work Experience:		
1984 to 1989	Employer: Turner and Walker, Engineering Ltd, 25 Ringinglow Road Sheffield W45 5DT	Duties: Trainee Accountant
1989 to 1996	Valiant Insurance, 46 Queen's Road, Sheffield T7F 3BB	Duties: Clerk, Account's Department

Special Interests:Ice skating, football, reading, music

References: Mrs. Martin, General Manager, Valiant Insurance, 46 Queen's Road Sheffield T7F 3BB

Mr. Turner, Partner, Turner and Walker Engineering Ltd., Ringinglow Road, Sheffield W45 5DT

Take a look at these two covering letters, the first is written in a poor style, the second is acceptable:

Dear Mrs James

I saw a job that you advertised in the newspaper last week. The job was for a clerk in the accounts department with you company.
I want to apply for the job because I'm very interested in this type of work and I have already trained to do such a job and I have over 3 years experience as you can see from my CV in a good firm that does the same kind of work as yours.
I think I would be good at the job because of what I have said and it would be good to work with a good company like yours. The money and holidays are also good.
If you want I can see you at an interview

Yours sincerely
Tom Grossly

Dear Mrs James

I wish to be taken into consideration as an applicant for the post of clerk in your accounts department, as advertised in the Birmingham Globe dated 12th April 19.. .
The reason for my application for the position is that I have in excess of three years experience employed by a company involved in the same area as Onions Ltd. As a result I am sure that I can contribute positively to your company. I would also be extremely keen to work for a well-established and respected firm such as yours. As can be seen from my CV I am fully qualified as an accounting clerk.
You will see that I give the names of two referees who will be happy to vouch for my abilities at work.
I would be pleased to have the opportunity of discussing my candidature with you at an interview.
Please do not hesitate to contact me if you have any queries regarding this application.

Yours sincerely
Martin Smart

(V) Vocabulary: To help you understand

ability	Fähigkeit
accountant	Buchhalter
accounts department	Buchhaltungsabteilung
advertise	annoncieren
advertisement	Anzeige, Annonce
applicant	Bewerber
application	Bewerbung
apply for	bewerben um
apply on spec	sich auf gut Glück bewerben
area	Gebiet
candidature	Kandidatur
certificate	Zeugnis
complete a form	ein Formular ausfüllen
consideration; take into ~	in Betracht ziehen
contribute	beitragen
covering letter	Begleitbrief
curious	neugierig
curriculum vitae (CV)	Lebenslauf
dated	datiert
duty	Pflicht
education	Ausbildung
employed	beschäftigt sein
employee	Arbeitnehmer
excess;in excess ~ of	über (mehr als)
experience	Erfahrung
fill in/complete	ausfüllen
form	Formular
GCE A Level	Abi
GCE O Level	mittlere Reife
hesitate	zögern
ice skating	Eislauf
impression	Eindruck
interview	Vorstellungsgespräch

involved	beteiligt
keen	sehr interessiert
post	Stelle
query	Frage
referee	Referenz
reference	Referenz (Zeugnis)
regarding	in bezug auf
respected	angesehen
response; in ~ to	in Antwort auf
situations vacant	Stellenangebote
spelling mistake	Rechtschreibfehler
submit	einreichen
untidy	unordentlich
vacancy	freie Stelle
vitals	lebenswichtige Organe
vouch for	sich verbürgen für
weed out	aussieben
well established	gut eingeführt

↔ Put It Another Way

I should like to apply for the position as...	Ich möchte mich um die Stelle als ... bewerben
please consider my application for the position as ...	Bitte ziehen Sie meine Bewerbung für die Stelle als ... in Betracht
I have been told that there is a vacancy in your department	ich habe erfahren, daß in Ihrer Abteilung eine Stelle frei ist
I am writing to enquire if you have an opening for a secretary	hiermit möchte ich anfragen, ob Sie eine freie Stelle für eine Sekretärin haben
I enclose my curriculum vitae as well as copies of certificates	ich füge meinen Lebenslauf sowie Kopien von Zeugnissen bei

at present I am employed as ... with Johnson Ltd.	augenblicklich bin ich als ... bei Johnson Ltd beschäftigt
the reason for my application is ...	der Grund für diese Bewerbung ist ...
I wish to work in a post with more responsibility	ich möchte eine Stelle mit mehr Verantwortung haben
I would like to widen my experiences and improve my prospects for promotion	ich möchte meine Erfahrungen erweitern und meine Aussichten auf Beförderung verbessern
I am at present unemployed	augenblicklich bin ich arbeitslos
my previous employer is willing to provide a reference for me	mein früherer Arbeitgeber ist bereit, eine Empfehlung für mich zu geben
I would be grateful if you sent me an application form	ich wäre dankbar, wenn Sie mir ein Bewerbungsformular schicken würden
I will be happy to attend an interview	ich würde gerne zu einem Vorstellungsgespräch kommen
I am available for interview by arrangement	ich bin für ein Vorstellungsgespräch nach Vereinbarung verfügbar
I look forward to hearing a positive reply from you	ich würde mich über eine positive Antwort freuen
I will be pleased to send any further information you may request	ich schicke Ihnen gern jede gewünschte Informationen

B Brain Work Fifty: A little translation work

Here is a covering letter but unfortunately the person writing it left some of it in German. Please try and translate the German into English. Use the phrases and vocabulary in this chapter to help you.

Dear Mrs Duffy

Ich möchte mich um die Stelle bewerben as accountant which was advertised in the Daily Echo dated 23rd November 19.. .
As you can see from my curriculum vitae *augenblicklich bin ich als Buchhalter bei Humble and Thwackit beschäftigt.*
Although I am happy here, *ich möchte eine Stelle mit mehr Verantwortung haben.* I would also like to widen my experiences *und meine Aussichten auf Beförderung verbessern.*
I will be pleased to send you *weitere* information and *ich bin für ein Vorstellungsgespräch nach Vereinbarung verfügbar.*
I look forward to receiving a positive reply from you.

Yours sincerely
Victoria Hope

B Brain Work Fifty One: Correct the spelling mistakes

Over to you. Have a try at correcting the spelling mistakes and typing errors in the application below. You or the secretary have had a really bad day. Here is a tip: there are twelve mistakes. Oh, and another tip: some of the mistakes are typically German!

Dear Sir

I would like you to take me into consideration vor the position of engineer in your engineering deplartmint , as advertised in the Birmingham Globe, dited 23rd March 19.. .
The reason for my Ablikation are that I have many years experience in this area and I am sure that I can positively contribute to your company.
I am very clean to work for your company which is very well established and respkted.
You will see that I give the names of two rfreees who will be happy to wouch for my abilities at work. I would be pleased to have the oppertuniti to discuss my candidature with you at an interwiew.
Blease do not hesitate to kontakt me if you have any queries rigardink this application.

Yours faithfully

19 Chapter

Going International

CONTENTS

Focus: doing business through agents
Dialogue: Onions discuss agency agreements
Drop Them a Line: Getting help from Chambers of Industry and Commerce
Put It Another Way: Alternative phrases
Brain Work: Pick the correct word and a quiz

Joke Time

One day Bob Onion noticed[1] that one of the secretaries had been making changes to letters he dictated[2].
"Miss Barnes, in future, please do what you are paid for and leave the thinking to me" said Onion and added "I would be most pleased if you wrote down exactly[3] what I said thank you."
Not long after a customer received a letter from Bob Onion and it went as follows: "Dear Mr Smythe – write that with a 'y' and stick[4] an 'e' at the end – the silly old idiot[5] thinks it makes him sound more important. In response to your letter dated ... what was it? Oh look it up yourself will you. Anyway , we can offer you as our most respected and reliable[6] agent in Scotland – well, as far as we know, because we haven't noticed you swindling[7] us – a percentage of ..., now how little can I offer him? 25%, no I'll try 15% and see if he says anything.
I hope this is acceptable – if not go jump in a lake[8].

Yours most sincerely blah blah blah."

1 bemerken 2 diktieren 3 genau 4 setzen 5 blöder alter Idiot 6 zuverlässig 7 betrügen 8 in einen See springen

Focus: Doing business through agents

Big companies have whole departments to deal with distribution and export of their products outside their domestic markets. Really large companies can produce in part or totally overseas through subsidiaries. Smaller companies will make use of agents who work for themselves, often for commission as a percentage of what they sell. Agents are useful because they are cheaper than employing people full time. They also know their own market and are familiar with local customs and are in a better position to do business in their own area.

Dialogue: Onions discuss agency agreements

Trying to expand into markets outside Britain has not been easy. The market for boilers and heating equipment is not saturated in Britain but Bob Onion (**BO**) is an ambitious boss and as he says "Don't put all your eggs in one basket". Here we find him talking to two of his sales managers, Gerry Murry (**GM**) and Ian Miller (**IM**)

BO: Sales have been good but I want to know about selling abroad.
IM: We just don't know local conditions in a lot of countries.
BO: Exactly, for example what about that agent in Jamaica? Williams was it? Mr Murry, you sent him £540 worth of heating equipment on a trial basis. Since then how much has he sold?
GM: She sir, I mean he is a she. He's, I mean, she's called Mrs Williams not Mr Will ...
BO: I don't care if he was an 'it', Mr or Mrs! How many pounds of business have we had?
GM: From Mrs Williams, in Jamaica?
BO: Yes, from Mrs Williams in Jamaica!
GM: Er, so far?
BO: Yes, since we sent the heating equipment after you met Mrs Williams at the trade fair in, eh, in the Bahamas, yes the Bahamas, wasn't it?
GM: In pounds?
BO: Yes, in pounds!

GM: None. She seemed very professional. It was all about chicken farms and since a lot of people eat chicken in Jamaica the demand for heating equipment in the hatcheries should be massive.

IM: May I make a suggestion? We had a lot of interest at the Frankfurt Trade Fair. How about contacting Chambers of Commerce in Germany and asking them to put us in touch with reliable companies that can market our equipment there? Oh yes, and we had a lot enquiries from that Chinese company that said they thought our equipment would sell well in China.

BO: At last, a sensible suggestion! Get the addresses and write letters straight away!

Drop Them A Line: Getting help from Chambers of Industry and Commerce

Dear Sirs

Our company produces a wide range of heating units suitable for home and industrial use. Please find enclosed illustrated literature describing our products.
So far we have mostly sold our equipment on the domestic market and to a limited extent in Russia. Due to our success we consider we would also find a ready market in your country.
We are now seeking agents to sell our products on your market.
The agent must be reliable and have considerable experience in marketing such products.
We would be very grateful if you could assist us in getting in touch with suitable and reputable businesses.

Your faithfully
Ian Miller

Not much later Onions received a reply to their letter from Germany:

Dear Mr Miller

The local Chamber of Industry and Commerce was kind enough to supply us with your address and literature describing the various types of heating units produced by your firm.

Our company is a leading importer and distributor of boilers and heating equipment of many years standing. As a consequence we have valuable connections in the trade and a small but experienced team of sales staff.
We have looked at your brochures and are convinced that there is a promising market waiting to be developed here. Can you please contact us to detail the terms on which you want us to represent you.
If your firm is prepared to grant us the agency we will spare no effort to promote the sale of your product.

Yours sincerely
Fritz Gruber

(V) Vocabulary: To help you understand

agency agreement	Vertretervertrag
agent	Vertreter
appoint	ernennen
appreciate	zu schätzen wissen
appreciative	dankbar
as a result of	als Folge
Chamber of Industry and Commerce	Industrie- und Handelskammer
consequence; as a ~	als Folge
consider	betrachten
considerable	beträchtlich
demand	Nachfrage
develop a market	einen Markt erschließen
distribution	Verteilung
distributor	Großhändler
domestic market	Binnenmarkt
due to	aufgrund, wegen
experience	Erfahrung
experienced	erfahren
furnish with something	mit etwas versorgen
grant an agency	eine Vertretung übertragen
grateful	dankbar

hatcheries	Hühnerfarm
hold the view that	der Ansicht sein
illustrated literature	Bildmaterial
keen on	stark interessiert an
leading	führend, wichtig
line	Branche
locate something	etwas finden
market a product	etwas auf den Markt bringen
opinion; be of the ~	der Meinung sein
overseas market	Überseemarkt
owing to	infolge
promote	fördern
prospect	Aussicht
provide with	mit etwas versorgen
put in touch/contact	in Verbindung setzen
range	Sortiment, Auswahl
ready market; find a ~	einen guten Markt finden
reliable	zuverlässig
reputable	seriös, solide
response; in ~ to your letter	in Beantwortung Ihres Briefes
saturated	gesättigt
spare no effort	keine Mühe scheuen
standing; of many years' ~	mit einem langjährigen guten Ruf
subsidiary	Tochtergesellschaft
success	Erfolg
suitable	geeignet
supply	beliefern
thorough	gründlich
trade	Handel, Geschäft
valuable	wertvoll
wide range	große Auswahl

Put it Another Way: Alternative phrases

if you are not already represented here we would be interested in ...	falls Sie hier noch nicht eine Vertretung haben, wären wir interessiert ...
we have acted as agents for Messrs ... for many years	wir waren viele Jahre als Agenten für die Firma ... tätig
with more than 20 years experience	mit einer Erfahrung von mehr als 20 Jahren
we have a thorough knowledge of the market	wir haben eine gründliche Marktkenntnis
we will increase our activities in the near future	wir werden unsere Tätigkeiten in der nahen Zukunft erweitern
we have branches in all major cities	wir haben Filialen in allen großen Städten
we wish to act as a sole agent	wir möchten als Alleinvertreter tätig sein
we already represent five leading companies	wir vertreten schon fünf führende Firmen
we have specialised in selling ...	wir sind auf den Verkauf von ... spezialisiert
we feel sure that we will have a successful relationship	wir sind sicher, daß wir eine erfolgreiche Geschäftsbeziehung haben werden

B Brain Work Fifty Two: Pick out the correct word

Have a try at the following Brain Work and put in one of the three possibilities to complete the sentences correctly.

branches relationships leading

1) The company has ... in all large cities

team | sole agent | opportunists
2) We wish to act as your ... here in Italy

electrical | valuable | detailed
3) This agency has ... connections in this line

leading | distributed | experienced
4) Our company is a/an ... importer of this equipment

sale | knowing | knowledge
5) We have a thorough ... of the local market

B Brain Work Fifty Three: Quiz time

Last but not least a small quiz on the chapter.

1) Agents are useful for:
a) production
b) selling
c) banking

2) Agents are often paid:
a) provisions
b) commission
c) deals

3) Knowledge of local markets is:
a) reputable
b) important for selling
c) important for banking

4) Large firms can produce overseas in their:
a) subsidiaries
b) departments
c) domestics

5) The English for "Erfolg" is:
a) follow
b) success
c) experience

6) Another word for the home market is the:
a) domestic market
b) overseas market
c) outside market

Shipping Goods

CONTENTS

Joke Time

Bob Onion met the boss of another company, Fred Potter, in the pub.
Onion: How's business?
Potter: Great! One of my people got an order for £160,000 last week.
Onion: £160,000! I just don't believe it!
Potter: It's totally true. Look, I've got the cancellation[1] right here.

1 Stornierung

Focus: Transport and shipping

Normally, details of how goods are to be shipped or forwarded are given in the order. For example details will be given on how the goods are packed. This depends on the type of goods and in part how the goods are transported. For example, perishable goods like food cannot be transported in the same way as machine parts, timber or coal. In the same way the means of transport is influenced by the type of goods, how soon the goods are needed and availability of cargo space. Clearly this can be a complex matter and is frequently put into the hands of specialists called forwarding agents and carriers. These people are very familiar with the problems of transport. They also get lower rates for shipping as they can send several different consignments together. They also provide shipping documents and arrange insurance and deal with customs. On the international level forwarding agents have offices in many countries and are easily in a position to transport goods efficiently.

Dialogue: Onions organise a shipment to China

Gerry Murry (**GM**) and Ian Miller (**IM**) are looking at the options for sending their equipment overseas. They have found an agent in China and they have received an order for boilers from this agent.

GM: I wrote to a couple of shipowners asking for quotations for their freight rates from Liverpool to Hong Kong.

IM: Hong Kong, really?

GM: Yes, the agent wants the boilers sent to Hong Kong and then they will distribute them by truck or train to China. I have a reply here from one shipowner (*reads the letter*)

Dear Sirs, we have received your enquiry of 29th April and can inform you that our current freight rate for boilers in crates, Liverpool to Hong Kong is £55 per metric tonne. We sail once a week. Hong Kong is our last port of call and the voyage takes twenty one days. (*stops reading*)

Now, my question is "what did they say in the order, when did they say they needed the boilers?"

IM: In four weeks.

GM: That's okay then. They sent a sailing card for cargo ship Enterprise and a shipping instruction form. I'll fill it in and send it back.

Drop Them A Line: Advice of despatch to Hong Kong

A week later Gerry Murry informs the customers that the order has been despatched:

Dear Sirs

Your Order No. 459/f of 3rd April 19..

We are pleased to inform you that the water heaters (boilers) ordered under the above order have been despatched as arranged.
The boilers are packed in 10 crates, 4 boilers to a crate. The crates are marked JGO in square, HONG KONG and are numbered 1–10.
The shipment is arriving in Hong Kong on 25th May, on the Enterprise, which sailed from Liverpool today.
Shipping document including bills of lading, commercial invoices, and insurance certificate, in triplicate have been sent together with our sight draft for £765, to Barclays Bank, Oxford St, in accordance with the letter of credit opened with them.
We are convinced that the boilers will prove to be satisfactory and we hope you will contact us again in the near future with new orders.

Yours faithfully
G. Murry.

Vocabulary: To help you understand

accordance; in ~ with	gemäß, entsprechend
availability	Vorrätigkeit
cargo	Fracht
coal	Kohle

commercial invoice	Handelsrechnung
consignment	Sendung
convinced; to be ~	sicher sein, überzeugt sein
crate	Kiste
customs	Zoll
despatch	versenden
enquiry	Anfrage
familiar	vertraut
fill in	ausfüllen
food	Nahrungsmittel
form	Formular
forward	befördern, senden
forwarding agent	Spediteur
freight rate	Frachtsatz
influence	beeinflussen
insurance	Versicherung
insurance certificate	Versicherungszertifikat
letter of credit	Akkreditiv
mark	beschriften
matter	Sache, Angelegenheit
number	numerieren
perishable	leicht verderblich
port of call	Anlaufhafen
rate	Satz
sail	auslaufen
ship	verschiffen/versenden
shipowner	Reederei
shipping documents	Versanddokumente
shipping instructions	Versandanweisungen
sight draft	Sichtwechsel
square	Viereck
timber	Holz, Bauholz
truck	Lastwagen

↔ Put it Another Way: Alternative Phrases

we want to charter a ship	wir möchten ein Schiff chartern
we need a ship with a cargo capacity of 5,000 tons	wir brauchen ein Schiff mit einer Ladekapazität von 5000 Tonnen
the ship must be ready for loading on 2nd November	das Schiff muß am 2. November ladebereit sein
we understand that you offer a global freight service	wir haben erfahren, daß Sie einen weltweiten Frachtdienst anbieten
your company operates a container service	Ihr Unternehmen unterhält einen Containerdienst
the goods will be packed in cartons	die Waren werden in Kartons verpackt
the cartons measure ... x ... x ...cm and weigh ... kg	Die Kartons haben die Abmessung ... x ... x ... cm und wiegen ... kg
please quote us your lowest rates	nennen Sie uns bitte Ihre niedrigsten Tarife
please let us have the times and frequency of your sailings	bitte teilen Sie uns mit, wann und wie oft die Route gefahren wird
please tell us the name of the next ship sailing to Tripoli and the deadline for accepting cargo	bitte nennen Sie uns den Namen des nächsten Schiffes nach Tripolis und den letzten Termin, an dem Ladungen angenommen werden
please deliver the goods at once/ not later than 4th march/by road/ by air	bitte beförden Sie die Waren sofort/ nicht später als 4. März/per Lastwagen/durch Luftfracht
please ensure the goods are not stored in the open	bitte sorgen Sie dafür, daß die Waren nicht im Freien gelagert werden
our packing instructions must be strictly observed	unsere Packanweisungen müssen genau beachtet werden

Brain Work Fifty Four: Translate some parts

Over to you! Please translate the parts of the letter left in German by a lazy colleague! Use the phrases in this chapter to help you.

Dear Sirs

We have *erfahren, daß Ihre Firma einen Containerdienst unterhält.*
Our company needs to send 54 diesel motors to Istanbul and we would like a quotation for your current *Frachtsätze. Die Waren werden in Kisten verpackt und haben die Abmessung 1 Meter 50 cm x 1 Meter 20 x 2 Meter und wiegen 1258 kg.*
Please let us have the times and frequency of you sailings *und nennen den Namen des Schiffes und den letzten Termin, an dem Ladungen angenommen werden.*

Yours faithfully

Letter Box: A few prepositions

Prepositions are always tricky. Here are some of the more important ones used in business letter writing. Note that with certain nouns and verbs we use certain prepositions.

in response to your letter	als Antwort auf Ihren Brief
in reply to your letter	als Antwort auf Ihren Brief
on examining the shipment	bei der Untersuchung der Sendung
we are interested **in** this model	wir interessieren uns für dieses Modell
we must insist **on** prompt delivery	wir müssen auf prompter Lieferung bestehen
the shipment consisted **of** 4 crates	die Sendung bestand aus 4 Kisten
we waited two weeks **for** the goods	wir warteten zwei Wochen auf die Waren

he will pay **by** cheque or **in** cash	er wird in bar oder mit Scheck bezahlen
delivery **by** van	Lieferung durch Lieferwagen
with reference **to** our previous correspondence	unter Bezugnahme auf unsere vorhergehende Korrespondenz

B Brain Work Fifty Five: Test your positions

Time to see if you can put in the prepositions. Use the information from the letter box to put in the correct prepositions.

1) All bills will be paid ... cheque.
2) We are writing to you ... response to your letter dated 12 June 19.. .
3) Our company is very interested ... this product.
4) ... examining the crates we saw that two were damaged.
5) Delivery will be ... train.
6) ... reference to our previous letter, we wish to point out that delivery must be prompt.

21 Chapter

Subsidiaries

CONTENTS

Joke Time

Onions is expanding. Bob Onion invited[1] five of his sales team into his office.
"You have all done so well with selling abroad that I'm giving you all a cheque for £1,500. If you keep working like this, I may even sign[2] it."

1 einladen 2 unterschreiben

Focus: Subsidiaries and branches

There are many advantages to having a branch or subsidiary abroad. Producing in a country close to the market means that you can reduce transport costs and all problems that can result from transporting goods. A subsidiary is a separate firm but its capital is controlled by the home company. A branch is part of the home company. Being close to a market also means you are more familiar with the needs of your customer, you know what they require and can change your product accordingly. You can avoid quotas and tariffs as your product is not imported. Depending on where a factory is set up, there are advantages with lower wages and lower costs in general. Local and national governments are willing to help with assistance such as cheap or even free factory space as well as financial incentives.
However, establishing a production facility in a foreign country can be risky and is very expensive because of the cost of investment.

Dialogue: Onions go to China

Bob Onion (**BO**) is talking to his main investor, Ted Cash (**TC**), and Ron Stuffy (**RS**) from Greyfellows Bank.

TC: The advantages are clear Bob, I can see that producing our boilers in China will be cheaper and there is a ready market there, but why China? It's so far away. And the risks!

BO: The sale of our boilers in China through our new agent in Hong Kong is, well, to be honest incredible. We just can't keep up with demand. You know we have transport costs and quotas to pay. Oh, and you haven't forgotten that little strike we had. Well, in the situation at the moment in a rapidly expanding market with lots of competition any hold up could be fatal. In China there will be no strike risk and no transport costs and no quotas.

RS: Yes, but there will be other costs. Massive investment.

BO: Do we have the money?

RS: Well yes, but ...

BO: There we are then!

TC: Not so fast, Bob! What about our sales in Germany and Eastern Europe? Didn't we sell a lot in Germany?

BO: We did, our equipment is cheap and efficient.

TC: So why not set up production there?

BO: You must be kidding! Think of the labour costs.

RS: Yes, according to our information it would cost 50% more to produce in Germany than even in Britain.

BO: What's more we have been told by our agent in Hong Kong that we will get a lot of help from the local government in Shanghai.

TC: Well, okay then. We will discuss this with other investors but I want to see on paper what's on offer and then we will go ahead.

BO: Great. I'll drop the ministry or council or whatever they are called in Shanghai a line to ask about what they can offer us.

TC: One other thing. I hope that this won't mean closing production here. This company has been making boilers here for years and it would sad to see all that change.

BO: Don't worry, demand here will stay high. Now, sorry gentlemen but I have a letter to write.

Drop Them a Line: An enquiry about a subsidiary

Bob Onion writes a letter to the Shanghai City Council to enquire about setting up a production facility in Shanghai:

Dear Sirs

We have obtained your address from your embassy in London. Our company is an expanding engineering business active in the area of heating equipment and water boilers.
As demand for our products is expanding in the Far East we are evaluating the best location of such a plant to satisfy demand both in China but also in neighbouring countries.
At present we are doing a lot of business with your country on an agency basis but demand is so great for our products that we are considering setting up a production plant in the Shanghai area. If conditions are positive we will look for a company there which will act as a joint owner

of a subsidiary. We wish to establish a full production plant together with distribution and service facilities.
We would be very pleased if you would send us information on industrial sites in the Shanghai area together with financial assistance and other incentives.
We are looking forward to hearing from you soon.

Yours sincerely
Robert Onion
Managing Director

(V) Vocabulary: To help you understand

abroad	im Ausland
accordingly	dementsprechend
advantage	Vorteil
area	Gebiet
assistance	Hilfe
avoid	vermeiden
branch	Filiale
close to	in der Nähe von
condition	Bedingung
consider	glauben
council	Verwaltung
demand	Nachfrage
depending on	hier: je nachdem
distribution	Verteilung
embassy	Botschaft
establish	gründen
evaluate	einschätzen, beurteilen
expanding	expandierend
facility	Einrichtung
in general	im allgemeinen
incentive	Anreiz
incredible	unglaublich
inspect	besichtigen

joint owner	Mitbesitzer
local government	Kommunalverwaltung
location	Lage, Örtlichkeit
look for	suchen nach
ministry	Ministerium
need	Bedürfnis
neighbouring	angrenzend, benachbart
obtain	bekommen, erhalten
plant	Anlage, Fabrik
quota	Kontingent
satisfy	zufriedenstellen
set up	gründen, einrichten
site	Gelände, Stelle, Grundstück
space	Platz, Raum
subsidiary	Tochtergesellschaft
tariff	Zoll
transport cost	Transportkosten
wage	Lohn
willing to	bereit zu

↔ Put It Another Way: Alternative phrases

if you move your company here there will be several advantages	wenn Sie Ihre Firma hierher verlegen, bieten sich mehrere Vorteile
there are good road and rail connections	es gibt gute Straßen- und Bahnverbindungen
the government will provide incentives	die Regierung wird Anreize bieten
sites are available for rent	Grundstücke können gepachtet werden
you can inspect the sites	Sie können die Grundstücke besichtigen

there are factory buildings available for immediate use	es gibt Fabriken, die zu sofortiger Nutzung zur Verfügung stehen
if you wish to expand your factory there will be no problem as there is building land adjoining	falls Sie Ihre Fabrik erweitern möchten, wird es kein Problem geben, da Bauplatz angrenzt
special loans are available	Sonderfinanzierungen werden gewährt

B Brain Work Fifty Six: Memory work

Over to you! Test your memory and see if can put the German and English words together

1) subsidiary	a) Einrichtung
2) set up	b) Kontingent
3) facility	c) Zoll
4) branch	d) gründen
5) quota	e) Filiale
6) tariff	f) Tochtergesellscaft

B Brain Work Fifty Seven: Quiz time

And now a quiz on expanding abroad. Good luck!

1) What is the difference between a subsidiary and a branch?

a) A subsidiary is a separate company and a branch is part of the home company

b) A subsidiary is part of the home company and a branch is a separate company

c) Both words mean the same; a company that has a factory abroad

2) Which of the following sentences from a letter is correct?

a) We have retained your address from the Italian Embassy

b) We have obtained your address from the Italian Embassy
c) We have obtained your adress from the Italian Embassy

3) In which area of business would we expect to hear about quotas and tariffs?
a) Production in a factory
b) The import and export of goods
c) The transport of goods in one country

4) The words 'set up' are used in the correct way in one of the sentences. Which?
a) A new factory was set up and a lot workers lost their jobs.
b) We wish to set up a factory in France
c) I'm sorry but I must set up your answer.

5) When two or more people own the same company they can be called
a) The company joints
b) The joint owners
c) The own jointers

6) If someone said 'you can inspect the site' you would expect to see
a) A type of chair
b) A place where things can be built or done
c) The doctor for an eye test

Thanks and Congratulations

CONTENTS

Joke Time

Bob Onion organised a meeting with his sales staff after his visit to China. The time for the meeting was 5 o'clock on Friday afternoon.
One of the managers said "Isn't a meeting at this time very inconvenient?[1]"
"Not at all," Onion answered, "it's very convenient for me. You see at that time and at that point[2] in the week nobody wants to argue[3] with me. It's very simple."

1 unbequem 2 Zeit 3 streiten

Focus: Maintaining good contacts

Mainly to create goodwill and maintain good business contacts, firms will send letters congratulating good and well-known clients and customers if they get promotion or perhaps even on a more personal level if someone you do business with gets married. There are also times when people in business need to say thank-you, for example, after a visit to a firm where they were looked after in some way by the employees in that company. Although this area is not vital to business, it is important as it creates a good atmosphere and perhaps paves the way for further business.

Dialogue: Good news all round at Onions

Bob Onion is meeting members of his sales team, Gerry Murry (**GM**), and Ian Miller (**IM**)after Bob Onion (**BO**) has just come back from a visit to their subsidiary in Shanghai.

IM: So, how was the trip and what's the situation in China?

BO: Wonderful, after we get the bureaucracy sorted out and other paper work it looks like things are looking up!

GM: What about the site and the work force?

BO: Well, we have a small factory on the edge of town. It's really new. We need to install all the machines and pay for telephone lines to the plant. I met some of the managers and the boss of the local firm, Wah Foo Ltd., who are the joint owners of the company. I was very impressed. With the reduced labour costs we can import some of our products back to Europe and make our activities here more competitive.

GM: And won't we need some of our people out there to keep an eye on things?

BO: That is my next point. Thanks to your activities, gentlemen, in developing contacts with the East, this whole deal has come to fruition. Since you, Gerry, have a lot of overseas experience, I have decided to send you over there as the manager. Promotion!

GM: Oh, really!

BO: Yes, a man of your experience will be vital, especially as things on the ground are a little, how should I put it? Yes, er, basic.

GM: Basic?! How basic?

BO: You know, Gerry, we are breaking new ground. I mean the accommodation.

GM: But didn't you say the accommodation was good, I mean you said you lived in the Shanghai Intercontinental, swimming pool, sauna, tennis courts and a three room suite?

BO: I did, but you will need to live close to the plant to keep a good grip on things. The factory is 50 kilometres out of Shanghai and transport being such a problem, well, you need to be there.

GM: So what's wrong with the accommodation there? Local three star hotel?

BO: The problem is there is no accommodation! But a flat is being built at the moment.

GM: When will it be ready?

BO: Well, you need to be out there next month, April and if all goes well the flat will be ready by July. The boss of Wah Foo Ltd. has provided an emergency solution.

GM: What kind of solution?

BO: A hut. It's a comfortable hut, I saw it myself. Oh and Ian, I want you to be head of sales with special responsibility for the Far East here at our plant in the UK.

IM: Thanks a lot, Mr Onion. I'm looking forward to working with Gerry on an international level.

BO: Okay, gentlemen, now that I've given you the good news I need to write a letter of thanks to Wah Foo for taking such good care of me while I was there.

Drop Them a Line: Letters of thanks and congratulations

Bob Onion, who knows all about good business, wrote a letter of thanks to the boss of the Chinese company, Mr Foo. Here it is.

Dear Mr Foo

Now that I am back in Britain I would like to take the opportunity of thanking you most warmly for the excellent hospitality you extended to me. It was indeed wonderful to have this possibility of meeting you and visiting your company and Shanghai prior to us starting in business together.
I am convinced that our co-operation will be long lasting and successful. I hope and look forward to being able to receiving a visit from you here in Britain in the near future.

I thank you once again, and I am

Sincerely yours,
Robert Onion

Ian Miller, having been promoted at Onions, was sent a letter from a customer in Germany, Mr Gruber:

Dear Mr Miller

It was with great pleasure that I was informed by Frau Dietz, our UK buyer, that you have been promoted to head of sales for the Far East. May I take the opportunity of congratulating you most sincerely on this promotion and wish you every success in the future?
With my personal regards

Yours sincerely
Fritz Gruber

(V) Vocabulary: To help you understand

accommodation	Unterkunft
all round	ringsum
basic	einfach, elementar
break new ground	Neuland erschließen
bureaucracy	Bürokratie
congratulation	Glückwunsch
convinced	überzeugt
create	erzeugen
edge	Rand
emergency solution	Notlösung
employee	Arbeitnehmer
excellent	ausgezeichnet
extend hospitality	Gastfreundschaft erweisen
flat	Wohnung
fruition; bring to ~	aufblühen lassen
goodwill	Wohlwollen
hospitality	Gastfreundlichkeit
hut	Hütte
impressed	beeindruckt
keep a good grip on	im Griff haben
keep an eye on	die Sache im Auge behalten
long lasting	lange während
look after	sich kümmern um
look up (things are looking up)	es geht bergauf
mainly	hauptsächlich
maintain	aufrechterhalten
pave the way	den Weg ebnen
pleasure	Freude
prior	bevor
promotion	Beförderung
sort out	erledigen
take the opportunity	die Gelegenheit ergreifen

virtually	fast
vital	sehr wichtig
warmly	herzlich
work force	Arbeitskraft

↔ To Put it Another Way: Alternative phrases

Saying thank you

this is just to thank you once again	hiermit möchte ich Ihnen nochmals danken
I want to thank you most sincerely	ich möchte Ihnen aufrichtig danken
I feel that this meeting was most beneficial to future business	ich denke, daß dieses Treffen für unsere zukünftigen Geschäfte sehr förderlich war
thank you very much for an excellent meal	ich danke Ihnen für eine ausgezeichnete Mahlzeit
I hope you will give me the opportunity of reciprocating before long	ich hoffe, daß Sie mir die Gelegenheit geben, mich bald erkenntlich zu zeigen

Congratulations

I am writing to convey my warm congratulations	ich möchte Ihnen herzlich gratulieren
this is a brief note to say "congratulations"	ich möchte Ihnen kurz gratulieren
I was pleased to learn of your promotion	ich habe mich gefreut, von Ihrer Beförderung zu erfahren

B Brain Work Fifty Eight: Correct the letter

Please take a look at this letter and find the mistakes made by someone in the office. Use Bob Onion's letter to help you. Oh yes, there are nine mistakes.

Dear Mr Peabody

This is to thank you mostly sincere and warmly for the excellent hospital you extended me.
It was indeed wonderful to have this possibility of to meeting you and your managers.
I hop and look forward to be able to receiving a visitor from you here in England.

Yours sincerely
Fred Dolittle

B Brain Work Fifty Nine: Put in the words

Over to you to put in the following words in the sentences below. Use the words and phrases in this chapter to help you.

a) reciprocating	b) extending	c) promotion
d) take	e) sincerely	f) pleasure

1) Thank you for ... your hospitality to me during my visit.
2) I want to thank you most ... for an excellent meal.
3) We were very pleased to learn of your ...
4) I now wish to ... the opportunity of thanking you.
5) It was with great ... that I learned of your promotion.
6) I hope that you will give me the opportunity of ... before long.

Key to Exercises

CHAPTER 1

Brain Work One

1) Thank you very much for
2) If we purchase in excess of
3) In addition to this
4) were of inferior quality
5) We will be forced to find
6) an alternative supplier
7) to provide us with the goods

Brain Work Two

1) Your sincerely
2) Dear Sir/Madam, Dear Sirs, Dear Sir or Madam
3) Yours faithfully
4) Dear Sir or Madam
5) (to start) Dear Mr Stecker, (to end) Yours sincerely

CHAPTER 2

Brain Work Three

1) Please inform us or Please let us know
2) If your prices are competitive or If your prices are favourable
3) If your goods come up to our expectations or If your goods meet with our approval
4) We saw your advertisement in ...
5) Please make us an offer for ...

Brain Work Four

a) – 4) grateful
b) – 5) concerning
c) – 7) quotation
d) – 9) enclosed
e) – 2) in addition
f) – 6) terms
g) – 8) substantial
h) – 3) competitive
i) – 1) approval

Brain Work Five

Please note that there are several possible answers to these exercises.

1) Could you please let us have/send us brochures about your tools?
2) Would it be possible for you to let us have your terms this week?
3) Could you please tell us what types of discounts you offer?
4) We were wondering if it might be possible for you to send us details about your wines and spirits?
5) Could/Would you please quote your prices c.i.f. Melbourne?
6) Could/Would you please let us have/send us delivery dates and discount details?

CHAPTER 3

Brain Work Six

The order of the sentences in the letter should be:

b) Dear Mr Wilson
d) We were pleased to receive your enquiry dated ...
e) As requested we are sending you a catalogue and price list
g) We are also pleased to grant you a discount of 10% for an early order
f) Please note that this offer and discount is valid for two weeks
c) We look forward to the pleasure of doing business with you
a) Yours sincerely

Brain Work Seven

1) – e), 2) – f), 3) – d), 4) – a), 5) – b), 6) – c)

Brain Work Eight

1) *We are* sending you information as requested
2) Your order *will* receive immediate attention
3) *We would* like a special discount
4) He *did not* send the letter on Tuesday
5) *It is* very expensive
6) The firm *has not* granted a discount

CHAPTER 4

Brain Work Nine

The order of the sentences in the letter should be:

1) f) Dear Mrs. Jackson
2) c) We were pleased to receive your quotation of 12th May
3) d) Kindly supply us with five kilos of first quality English Tea
4) e) Please arrange an early delivery and notify us as soon as the goods are shipped
5) b) We shall place further orders with you if this order is satisfactorily executed
6) a) Yours sincerely

Brain Work Ten

1) – c), 2) – f), 3) – b), 4) – g), 5) – a), 6) – d)

Brain Work Eleven

1) payable, 2) quotation, 3) point, 4) place, 5) irrevocable, 6) satisfaction

CHAPTER 5

Brain Work Twelve

1) – f), 2) – g), 3) – a), 4) – e), 5) – b), 6) – d), 7) – c)

Brain Work Thirteen

1) sufficient, 2) advise, 3) payment, 4) consignment, 5) successful
6) delivery

Brain Work Fourteen

a) – 3, b) – 5, c) – 4, d) – 8, e) – 6, f) – 2, g) – 7, h) – 1

CHAPTER 6

Brain Work Fifteen

1) This firm is not *competitive*
2) We will *despatch/send/ship/forward* the goods within 5 days
3) We want to *apologise* for the delay in the *execution* of your order
4) Industrial action resulted in a *delay*
5) *Order books* are so full that the workers are doing overtime
6) We are *forced* to ask for an extension of the delivery time

Brain Work Sixteen

1) sorry, 2) executing, 3) delay, 4) damaged, 5) position, 6) assure
7) despatch

Brain Work Seventeen

1) – c, 2) – a, 3) – a, 4) – b, 5) – b, 6) – a

CHAPTER 7

Brain Work Eighteen

1) – c), 2) – a), 3) – d), 4) – f), 5) – e), 6) – b)

Brain Work Nineteen

1) attach, 2) instructed, 3) execute, 4) valid, 5) confirmed

Brain Work Twenty

1) enclosing, 2) instructed, 3) open, 4) irrevocable, 5) valid, 6) confirmed,
7) agent

Brain Work Twenty One

1) F, 2) T, 3) T, 4) F

CHAPTER 8

Brain Work Twenty Two

The order of the sentences in the letter should be:

2) Dear Mr Free
6) We should like to remind you that payment for order No 439B is a month overdue
4) Please find a copy of your invoice attached
5) An early settlement of this account would be appreciated
1) We look forward to hearing from you in the next few days
7) If you have already sent a remittance please disregard this letter
5) Yours sincerely

Brain Work Twenty Three

1) F, 2) F, 3) T, 4) T, 5) F

Brain Work Twenty Four

1) Payment was due a month ago
2) Could you please clear/pay your account as soon as possible?
3) Please disregard/ignore this letter if you have already cleared the account
4) Thank you for the settlement/payment of the bill
5) The invoice has not yet been paid
6) Please see the attached account

CHAPTER 9

Brain Work Twenty Five

1) reminders, 2) insist, 3) solicitor, 4) Regrettably, 5) outstanding
6) remittance

Brain Work Twenty Six

1) remittance – Zahlung, 2) concerning – bezüglich,
3) delay – Verzögerung, 4) outstanding – ausstehend,
5) unless – es sei denn

Brain Work Twenty Seven

1) – b), 2) – b), 3) – b), 4) – b)

Brain Work Twenty Eight

1) by , 2) until, 3) until, 4) by, 5) by

CHAPTER 10

Brain Work Twenty Nine

1) – c), 2) – d), 3) – b), 4) – e), 5) – f), 6) – a)

Brain Work Thirty

1) receive, 2) beyond, 3) enclose, 4) inconvenience, 5) assure

Brain Work Thirty One

We regret very much the delay in payment of your *invoice/bill* No B527 for £102.50. The reason for the *delay/hold up* is that *we are having difficulties* because our *customers have recently been slow to meet their obligations.*
We *assure* you that our *present/current difficulties* are only *temporary* and that we will clear the *outstanding* amount *by the end of this month.*
Yours faithfully

CHAPTER 11

Brain Work Thirty Two

1) – b), 2) – c), 3) – a), 4) – c), 5) – b)

Brain Work Thirty Three

The order of the sentences in the letter should be:

2) We are forced to complain about the delay in our order No D546.
4) You assured us that the goods would be here within a week.
1) That was three weeks ago.
5) The delay puts us in a difficult position as we need the goods urgently.
3) We will be compelled to cancel the consignment if the goods do not arrive by next week.
6) We will be pleased to receive your explanation.

CHAPTER 12

Brain Work Thirty Four

1) convenient – passend, 2) grateful – dankbar,
3) opportunity – Möglichkeit 4) although – obwohl,
5) arrival – Ankunft, 6) prior to – vor/bevor

Brain Work Thirty Five

Dear Mr Barker
I would welcome the opportunity to meet you some time next week. *Would 10 o'clock on Tuesday be convenient? If* this day and time are not convenient *please suggest an alternative time and day.* Please contact me in the company. If I am out *a message will reach me in the office.*
I am looking forward to meeting you again.
Your sincerely

Brain Work Thirty Six

1) in, 2) on, 3) at, 4) in, 5) in, 6) on, 7) at

CHAPTER 13

Brain Work Thirty Seven

1) – b), 2) – d), 3) – e), 4) – f), 5) – a), 6) – c)

Brain Work Thirty Eight

1) Unfortunately, 2) convenient, 3) kind, 4) Owing, 5) afraid, 6) expect

Brain Work Thirty Nine

1) invitation – Einladung
2) opportunity – Möglichkeit
3) response – Antwort
4) overseas – Übersee
5) accommodation – Unterkunft
6) performance – Leistung

CHAPTER 14

Brain Work Forty

1) point out, 2) upon, 3) mistake, 4) Instead, 5) inconvenience, 6) as soon as

Brain Work Forty One

1) – a), 2) – b), 3) – a), 4) – b), 5) – a), 6) – b)

CHAPTER 15

Brain Work Forty Two

1) reference, 2) slip, 3) information, 4) reliable, 5) consider, 6) grant, 2) discretion, 8) assistance

Brain Work Forty Three

1) previous – vorherig/vorhergehend
2) standing – Ruf
3) recent – neulich
4) solvency – Zahlungsfähigkeit
5) confidential – vertraulich
6) creditworthy – kreditwürdig

Brain Work Forty Four

1) T, 2) F, 3) F, 4) F, 5) F, 6) T

CHAPTER 16

Brain Work Forty Five
1) – c), 2) – f), 3) – d), 4)– e , 5) – a), 6) – b)

Brain Work Forty Six
1) – b), 2) – f), 3) – c), 4) – g), 5) – e), 6) – d), 7) – h), 8) – a)

Brain Work Forty Seven
1) – a), 2) – b), 3) – c), 4) – a), 5) – a), 6) – c)

CHAPTER 17

Brain Work Forty Eight
We are writing to ask *you to grant us a loan of £20,000 for 12 months/for a period of 12 months.*
We need/require the loan to buy new machines for our factory. We are sure that as *customers* of many years you will agree we are a creditworthy company.
As security we can offer you share certificates worth £25,000.
If you wish to discuss the *matter, I would be ready* to visit you *at the bank.*
Yours faithfully

Brain Work Forty Nine
1) overdraft – Überziehung, 2) account – Konto,
3) current account – laufendes Konto, 4) transfer – überweisen,
5) loan – Darlehen, 6) cheque – Scheck

CHAPTER 18

Brain Work Fifty
Dear Mrs Duffy
I wish to apply for the post as accountant which was advertised in the Daily Echo dated 23rd November 19.. . As you can see from my curriculum vitae *I am, at present/currently, employed as an accountant at Humble and Thwackit.* Although I am happy here, *I wish to apply for a post with more responsibility.* I would also like to widen my experiences a*nd improve my prospects for promotion.*

I will be pleased to send you *further* information and *I am available for interview by arrangement.*
Yours sincerely
Victoia Hope

Brain Work Fifty One
deplartmint – department
dited – dated
Ablikation – application
clean – keen
respkcted – respected
rfreees – referees
wouch – vouch
oppertuniti – opportunity
interwiew – interview
Blease – Please
kontakt – contact
rigardink – regarding

CHAPTER 19

Brain Work Fifty Two
1) branches, 2) sole agent, 3) valuable, 4) experienced, 5) knowledge

Brain Work Fifty Three
1) – b), 2) – b), 3) – b), 4) – a), 5) – b), 6) – a)

CHAPTER 20

Brain Work Fifty Four
Dear Sirs
We have *found/learnt that your firm offers a container service.*
Our company needs to send 54 diesel motors to Istanbul and we would like a quotation for your current *freight rates. The goods are packed in crates and measure 1 meter 50 cm x (by) 1 meter 20 cm x (by) 2 meters and weigh 1258 kg.* Please let us have the times and frequency of your sailings *and please let us have the name of the ship and the last date/deadline for accepting cargo.*
Yours faithfully

Brain Work Fifty Five

1) by, 2) in, 3) in, 4) on, 5) by, 6) with

CHAPTER 21

Brain Work Fifty Six

1) – f), 2) – d), 3) – a), 4) – e), 5) – b), 6) – c)

Brain Work Fifty Seven

1) – a), 2) – b), 3) – b), 4) – b), 5) – b), 6) – b)

CHAPTER 22

Brain Work Fifty Eight

Dear Mr Peabody

This is to thank you most sincerely and warmly for the excellent hospitality you extended to me.

It was indeed wonderful to have this possibility of meeting you and your managers.

I hope and look forward to being able to receive a visit from you here in England.

Yours sincerely

Fred Dolittle

Brain Work Fifty Nine

a) – 6), b) – 1), c) – 3), d) – 4), e) – 2), f) – 5)

Letter Functions

Die englische Sprache ist sehr reich an Ausdrücken gleicher oder ähnlicher Bedeutung. Deshalb finden Sie in diesem systematischen Überblick für einen deutschen Satz oft mehrere englische Sätze. Außerdem ist es nicht immer möglich, eine deutsche Entsprechung für alle englischen Redemittel zu finden.

Briefe beginnen

Besten Dank für Ihren Brief vom ... mit der Anfrage über ...	*Many thanks for your letter dated ... with the enquiry about ...* *Thanks a lot for your letter of ... enquiring about ...*
Vielen Dank für Ihren Brief vom ... mit der Mitteilung, daß ...	*Thank you for your letter dated ...* *1) advising us that ...* *2) informing us that ...* *3) with the information that ...* *4) telling us that ...*
Wir danken Ihnen für Ihren Brief vom ... mit der beigefügten Preisliste	*We thank you for your letter of ...* 1) *with the enclosed price list* *2) enclosing your price list*

Wir bedauern sehr, Ihrem Schreiben vom ... zu entnehmen, daß ...	*We are extremely sorry to learn from your letter dated ... that ...*
Es freut uns zu hören, daß ...	*We are pleased to hear that ...* *1) We are happy to hear that ...* *2) We are glad to hear that ...*
Wir entnehmen Ihrem Brief vom ..., daß ...	*We note from your letter dated ... that ...*
Im Anschluß an meinen Brief vom ... sende ich Ihnen ...	*Further to my letter of ... I am sending you ...*
Mit Bezug auf unseren vorhergehenden Brief möchten wir darauf hinweisen, daß ...	*Refering to our previous letter, we wish to point out that...* **or** *With reference to our previous correspondance, we should like to point out that ...*
Wie ich in meinem vorigen Brief erwähnt habe ...	*As I mentioned in my previous letter ...*
In unserem letzten Brief vom ... haben wir erklärt, daß...	*In our last letter, dated ..., we explained that ...*

Briefe beenden

Wir hoffen, in der nahen Zukunft/ Kürze/bald/so bald wie möglich von Ihnen zu hören	*We look forward to hearing from you in in the near future/shortly/soon/as soon as possible.*
Ich hoffe, bald von Ihnen zu hören.	*We hope to hear from you shortly*
Wir wären sehr dankbar, von Ihnen so bald wie möglich zu hören	*We would be extremely grateful to hear from you as soon as possible* **or** *We would be very thankful if you contacted us as soon as possible*
Ich würde eine sofortige Antwort sehr schätzen.	*A prompt reply would be much/ greatly appreciated* **or**

	I would/should appreciate a prompt reply.
Dürfen wir bald von Ihnen hören?	*May we hear from you soon?* **or** *We trust we will hear from you shortly*
Da diese Sache äußerst eilig ist, antworten Sie uns bitte innerhalb der nächsten Tage.	*As this matter is very/extremely urgent please/kindly let us have a reply/an answer within the next few days.* **or** *Since this is a matter of great/extreme urgency would you please reply/ answer within the next few days.*
Bitte behandeln Sie diese Sache als äußerst dringend.	*Please treat this matter with the greatest urgency/utmost urgency.*
Antworten Sie uns bitte unbedingt bis nächsten Dienstag.	*Kindly let us have your reply by next Tuesday without fail*
Wir wären für eine Antwort möglichst/ spätestens bis zum ... dankbar	*We would appreciate an answer by ... if possible/at the latest.*

Anfragen

Bitte nennen Sie uns Ihre Preise für...	*Please quote your prices for ...*
Bitte schicken Sie uns Ihre äußersten Preise für ...	*Please quote your best/keenest/ lowest prices for ...*
Bitte schicken Sie uns weitere Einzelheiten über ...	*Please let us have further in formation about/concerning ...*
Können Sie ab Lager liefern?	*Can you supply from stock?*
Können Sie uns sofort ... liefern?	*Are you able to supply us with ... straight away?* 1) *Can you deliver 50 corduroy caps immediately?* 2) *Are you in a position to let us have ... without delay?*

Machen Sie uns bitte ein Angebot über ... und nennen Sie den frühesten Liefertermin.	*Please let us have a quotation for ... and the earliest date of delivery.* ***or*** *Would you please quote for ... stating/giving the earliest delivery date.*
Sie wurden uns von ... empfohlen.	*You have been recommended to us by ...*
Vorausgesetzt, daß Ihre Preise angemessen/günstig sind, ...	*Provided that your prices are reasonable/ favourable ...*
Wenn Ihre Preisangabe konkurrenzfähig ist, wären wir zu einem großen Auftrag/Probeauftrag bereit.	*If your quotation is competitive,we would be prepared to place a substantial/trial order.*
Wir beabsichtigen einen Auftrag zu erteilen, falls die Qualität der Waren unseren Erwartungen entspricht.	*We intend to place an order if the quality of the goods meets/comes up to our expectations/requirements.*
Wir benötigen ...	*We require/need ...* *1) We have a requirement for ...* *2) We have a need for ...*
Wir haben von ... erfahren, daß Sie ... herstellen.	*We have heard from ... that you produce ...*
Wir sind daran interessiert, ... zu importieren.	*We are interested in importing ...*
Wir wären sehr dankbar für die Zusendung Ihres neuesten Katalogs und ausführlicher Informationen über ...	*We should/would be very grateful if you could send/forward us your latest catalogue and detailed information about ...*
Wir werden einen großen Auftrag erteilen, wenn die Qualität der Waren zufriedenstellend ist.	*We will place a large order if the quality of the goods is satisfactory.*
Wir würden gerne Ihre neueste Preisliste und Exportbedingungen erhalten.	*We would/should be glad/pleased to recieve your most up to date/latest/ current price list and export conditions.*

Angebote	
Bitte beachten Sie, daß alle Preise einem Rabatt von ... Prozent unterliegen	*Please note that all prices are subject to a discount of ... per cent.*
Beiliegend senden wir Ihnen vollständige Angaben über Preise, Mengen, Verkaufsbedingungen sowie über Liefertermine.	*Enclosed you will find full information/ details about/concerning prices, quantities, conditions/terms of sale as well as delivery dates.*
Unsere Preise schließen Verpackung und Transport ein.	*Our prices include packing and carriage.*
Unsere Preise verstehen sich FOB ...	*Our prices are quoted FOB ...*
Wir entnehmen sehr gerne Ihrem Schreiben, daß Sie sich für unsere Geräte interessieren.	*We are pleased to learn from your letter that you are interested in our devices.*
Wir gewähren einen Rabatt von ... Prozent	*We grant a discount of ... per cent*
Wir haben uns sehr über Ihre Anfrage von ... gefreut.	*We were very pleased to recieve your offer of ...* *1) It was with great/considerable pleasure that we recieved your offer of ...* *2) We were extremely glad to recieve your offer dated ...*
Wunschgemäß senden wir Ihnen gerne den Katalog mit Einzelheiten über ...	*We are sending you, as requested/ desired our catalogue containing details about ...*
Dieses Angebot ist unverbindlich.	*This offer is without engagement*
Dieses Angebot ist gültig/fest für ...	*This offer is firm/valid for ...*
Wir versichern Ihnen, daß Ihr Auftrag zu Ihrer vollen Zufriedenheit ausgeführt wird.	*We assure/wish to assure you that* ***or*** *You may rest assured that your order will be executed/performed/carried out to your entire satisfaction.*

Sie können sich auf die sorgfältige Ausführung Ihres Auftrags verlassen.	*You can/may rely on the careful execution/performance of you order*
Wir freuen uns darauf, mit Ihnen ins Geschäft zu kommen.	*We look forward to doing business with you.*

Aufträge

Bitte bestätigen Sie den Erhalt dieses Auftrags.	*Please acknowledge this order.*
Bitte liefern Sie uns die nachstehend einzeln aufgeführten Waren:	1) *Please supply us with* 2) *Please let us have* 3) *Kindly send us the goods specified below.*
Bitte stornieren Sie den Auftrag.	*Please cancel the order.*
Die Qualität der Waren muß mit der der gelieferten Muster übereinstimmen.	*The quality of the goods must correspond to/be in accordance with that of the samples submitted/supplied.*
Ich hoffe, daß Sie diesen Auftrag pünktlich erledigen werden.	*I hope/trust you will execute this order in good time.*
Liefern Sie mir bitte die folgenden Artikel postwendend:	*Please supply me with the following goods by return:*
Wir bedauern, unseren Auftrag Nummer ... stornieren zu müssen.	*We regret having to cancel order number ...* 1) *We are sorry being forced/compelled to cancel our order number ...* 2) *We regret that we must cancel order number ...*
Wir danken Ihnen für Ihr Angebot von ... und bitten Sie um die Lieferung von ...	*We thank you for your offer dated ... and would be pleased if you would supply ...*
Wir hoffen, daß diese nur die erste von vielen Bestellungen sein wird.	*We trust/hope that this will be the first of many orders.*

Wir möchten Sie daran erinnern, daß unsere Kunden um sofortige Lieferung gebeten haben.	*We would/should like to remind you that our custmers requested immediate delivery.*
Wir müssen darauf aufmerksam machen, daß sorgfältige Verpackung unbedingt erforderlich ist.	*We must point out that careful packing is essential.* ***or*** *We must draw your attention to the fact that the careful packing of the goods is of great importance.*
Wir sind, wenn auch ungern, gezwungen, die Bestellung zu stornieren.	*It is with great reluctance that we are compelled to cancel the order.* ***or*** *We are reluctanty forced to cancel the order.*

Auftragsbestätigungen

Die Waren werden in wenigen Tagen abgesandt werden.	*The goods will be sent/despatched within a few days.*
Vielen Dank für Ihren Auftrag.	*Many thanks for your order.*
Wir bedauern, daß wir nicht in der Lage sind, die von Ihnen bestellten Waren zu liefern.	*We regret that we cannot supply/deliver the goods you ordered.*
Wir danken Ihnen für Ihre Bestellung, erteilt am ...	*We thank you for your order placed on ...*
Wir hoffen, daß dies der erste von vielen Aufträgen sein wird.	*We hope/trust that this will be the first of many orders.*
Wir sind sicher, daß Sie voll zufrieden mit der Ausführung Ihres Auftrags sein werden.	*We are/feel confident/sure/certain that you will be absolutely/completely/fully satisfied with the execution of your order.*
Wir werden uns sehr bemühen, die Fertigung Ihres Auftrags rechtzeitig zu erfüllen.	*We will do our best/utmost to complete the order in good time.*

Leider führen wir diesen Artikel nicht mehr.	*Unfortunately we no longer stock this item.*
Leider sind wir nicht in der Lage, die bestellten Waren zu liefern.	*Unfortunately, we are unable/not in a position to supply the goods you ordered.* **or** *We regret being unable to supply the goods ordered by you.*

Lieferungen und Verzögerungen

Wir können sofort versenden, da alle Waren ab Lager lieferbar sind.	*We can deliver at once as/since all goods are available from stock*
Wir können keinen sofortigen Versand garantieren, da viele Waren knapp sind.	*We are unable to guarantee immediate delivery/despatch as many goods are in short supply.*
Wir möchten Ihnen versichern, daß wir alles tun, um Ihren Auftrag auf den Weg zu bringen.	*We wish to assure you that we are doing everything/all in our power to despatch your order.*
Die Lieferung kann vor ... erfolgen	*We can effect delivery before ...*
Wir sind in der Lage, die Lieferung mit unseren Lastwagen/Lieferwagen zu arrangieren.	*We are able to/can arrange shipment/ delivery by our truck/van.*
Wir können die Sendung per Bahn innerhalb von ... nach Auftragserteilung liefern.	*We could send/ship the consignment by rail within ... of receiving your order.* **or** *It would be possible for us to forward the shipment within four days of receipt of your order.*
Wir freuen uns, Ihnen mitteilen zu können, daß die ... heute mit der Bahn versandt wurden.	*We are pleased/happy to inform/advise you that the ... have been despatched by rail/train today.*
Wir bedauern, Ihnen mitteilen zu müssen, daß ...	*We regret having to tell/inform you that ...*

Wir bedauern wirklich ...	*We are really/indeed sorry ...*
Bitte nehmen Sie unsere Entschuldigung entgegen.	*Please accept our appologies.*
Unsere Lieferanten waren nicht imstande, mit den Aufträgen Schritt zu halten.	*Our suppliers found it impossible/ were unable to keep up/pace with orders.*
Die Nachfrage war so groß, daß ...	*Demand was so great that ...*
Unsere Vorräte sind erschöpft.	*Our stock has been exhausted/used up.*
Ein Feuer hat unsere Fabrik beschädigt.	*A fire has damaged our plant.*
Wir hoffen, daß Sie unsere Lage verstehen.	*We trust/hope you will appreciate/ understand our position.*
Wir hoffen, daß diese Verzögerung Ihnen keine wesentlichen Unannehmlichkeiten verursachen wird.	*We hope/trust that this delay will not cause you inconsiderable inconvenience.*

Transport

Bitte befördern Sie die Waren sofort/ nicht später als .../per Lastwagen/ durch Luftfracht.	*Please deliver the goods at once/ not later than .../ by road/by air.*
Bitte nennen Sie uns den Namen des nächsten Schiffes nach ... und den letzten Termin, an dem Ladungen angenommen werden.	*Please inform us as to the name of the next ship sailing to ... and the deadline for accepting cargo.*
Bitte sorgen Sie dafür, daß die Waren nicht im Freien gelagert werden.	*Please ensure that the goods are not stored in the open.*
Bitte teilen Sie uns mit, wann und wie oft die Route gefahren wird.	*Please let us have the times and frequency of your sailings.*
Das Schiff muß am ... ladebereit sein.	*The ship must be ready for loading on ...*
Die Kartons haben die Abmessung ... und wiegen...	*The cartons measure ... and weigh ...*

Die Waren werden in Kartons verpackt.	*The goods will be packed in cartons.*
Ihr Unternehmen unterhält einen Containerdienst.	*Your company operates a container service.*
Nennen Sie uns bitte Ihre niedrigsten Tarife.	*Please quote us your lowest rates.*
Unsere Packanweisungen müssen genau beachtet werden.	*Our packing instructions must be strictly observed.*
Wir brauchen ein Schiff mit einer Ladekapazität von ... Tonnen.	*We require/need a ship with a cargo capacity of ... tons.*
Wir haben erfahren, daß Sie einen weltweiten Frachtdienst anbieten.	*We understand that you offer a global freight service.*
Wir möchten ein Schiff chartern.	*We want to charter a ship.* **or** *We wish to charter a vessel.*
Wir werden uns um die Zollabfertigung kümmern	*We will deal with the customs formalities ourselves.* **or** *We will attend to the customs formalities ourselves.*

Zahlung und Mahnungen

Unsere Zahlungsbedingungen sind: ...	*Our terms of payment are as follows: ...*
Vorauszahlung	*Cash in advance*
Per Nachnahme	*Cash on delivery/COD*
Zahlung bei Erhalt der Rechnung	*Payment on receipt of invoice*
Zahlung bei Erhalt der Waren	*Payment on receipt of goods*
Zahlung durch Bankwechsel	*Payment by bankerís draft*
... Tage netto	*... Days net*

Durch Wechsel mit ... Tagen Ziel	*By bill of exchange, at ... days*
Ich sehe dem Empfang Ihrer Zahlung über den Betrag entgegen.	*I look forward to receiving your payment of the amount.*
Die Waren sind in gutem Zustand angekommen.	*The goods arrived in good condition.*
Ich danke Ihnen für Ihre Lieferung und füge einen Scheck über den Betrag Ihrer Rechnung bei.	*I thank you for your delivery and I enclose a cheque covering the amount of your invoice.*
Wir haben den Betrag auf Ihr Konto in ... überwiesen.	*We have transfered the amount/sum to your account in ...*
Wir haben Zahlung in Höhe von ... durch die ... Bank in ... vorgenommen.	*We have arranged payment through the ... Bank in ... for the amount of ...*
Wir stellen mit Bedauern fest, daß ...	*We note with regret that ...* ***or*** *It is with regret that we note that ...*
Es ist schwer zu verstehen warum ...	*We are at a loss to understand ...*
Wir können es nicht verstehen, warum Sie unsere Schreiben unbeantwortet ließen.	*We fail to understand why you have not replied to our letter.* ***or*** *We do not understand the reason for your failure to answer our letter.*
Trotz wiederholter dringender Bitten um Begleichung unserer Rechnung haben wir noch immer nichts von Ihnen gehört.	*Despite/inspite of repeated urgent requests for payment of our invoice we have still received no reply from you.* ***or*** *Even though we have repeatedly sent you urgent requests for payment, we have yet to hear from you.*
Sie werden sicher verstehen, daß wir nicht länger auf Bezahlung warten können.	*You will surely appreciate the fact that we can wait no longer for payment.* ***or***

	You must clearly understand that we cannot be expected to wait any longer for payment.
Wir müssen auf Zahlung bestehen.	*We must insist on payment.*
Wir wären sehr dankbar für einen baldigen Ausgleich unserer Rechnung.	*Could you please settle our invoices as soon as possible.* ***or*** *We would appreciate an early settlement of our invoice very much.*
Wir werden unsere Rechtsanwälte anweisen, gerichtliche Schritte gegen Sie einzuleiten.	*We will instruct our solicitors to start proceedings/take legal action against you.*
Falls wir Ihren Scheck nicht innerhalb der nächsten ... erhalten, müssen wir die Angelegenheit unserem Rechtsanwalt übergeben.	*Unless we receive your cheque within the following ... we see ourselves compelled to put the matter in the hands of our solicitor.* ***or*** *Should we not be in receipt of your cheque within the next ... days we will be forced to turn the matter over to our solicitor.*
Bitte prüfen Sie den Kontoauszug und teilen Sie es uns mit, wenn Sie irgendwelche Unstimmigkeiten finden.	*Please check the statement and inform us if there any discrepancies.*

Antworten auf Mahnungen

Wir bedauern es sehr, nicht auf Ihre Briefe geantwortet zu haben.	*We regret very much not having replied to your letters.*
Wir bitten um Entschuldigung wegen der Verzögerung in der Beantwortung Ihrer Briefe vom ...	*We wish to apologize for the delay in answering your letters dated ...*

Es scheint, daß wir Ihre Zahlungsbedingungen nicht völlig verstanden haben.	*It would appear that we have not fully understood your terms of payment*
Es tut uns äußerst leid, daß Sie auf die Zahlung warten mußten.	*We are extremely sorry that you were forced to wait for payment.* ***or*** *We are very sorry indeed that you had to wait for payment.*
Heute haben wir unsere Bank angewiesen, die Summe von ... auf Ihr Konto zu überweisen	*We have today instructed our Bank to transfer ... to your account.*
Wir fügen einen Scheck über ... zum vollen Ausgleich Ihrer Rechnung bei.	*Please find enclosed a cheque for ... in full settlement of your bill.*
Infolge unvorhersehbarer Umstände war es uns unmöglich, Ihre letzte Rechnung laut dem Auftrag zu begleichen.	*As a consequence of circumstaces entirely beyond our control we were unable to settle your invoice in accordance with the order.*
Wir bedauern sehr, Sie um Aufschub bitten zu müssen.	*We regret having to request a respite.*
Angesichts unserer Schwierigkeiten müssen wir Sie um eine Kreditverlängerung bitten.	*In view of our problems, we are forced to ask for an extension of credit.*
Unsere gegenwärtigen Schwierigkeiten sind nur vorübergehend.	*Our current/present difficulties are only of a temporary nature.*
Unsere Kunden kommen in letzter Zeit ihren Verpflichtungen schleppend nach.	*Recently our customers have been slow in meeting their obligations.*
Wir haben erhebliche Schwierigkeiten beim Einzug unserer Rechnungen.	*We are experiencing great difficulty in collecting payment.*
Das Geschäft geht schlecht.	*Business has been slack.*
Wir sind in Schwierigkeiten gekommen, weil unser Hauptkunde Konkurs gemacht hat.	*We are in difficulties as our main customer has gone bankrupt.*

Wir beabsichtigen, die Rechnung bis zum Ende des Monats zu begleichen.	*We intended to pay the bill by the end of the month.*
Wir werden die ausstehende Summe bis Ende dieses Monats begleichen.	*We will clear the outstanding amount by the end of this month*
Wir werden alle Anstrengungen unternehmen, um die Rechnung bis Ende ... zu bezahlen.	*We are making every effort to pay the bill by the end of ...* ***or*** *We are doing our utmost to settle the account by the end of ...*
Wir bitten Sie, so freundlich zu sein, und uns noch einige Wochen bis zur Zahlung des Betrags zu gewähren.	*Please be good enough to grant us a few further weeks in which to pay the amount.*

Beschwerden

Wir müssen Ihnen leider mitteilen, daß ...	*We are unfortunately forced to inform you that ...* *1) Unfortunately, we have to tell you that ...* *2) We regret to inform you that ...* *3) Regretably, we must advise you that ...*
Leider müssen wir wegen ... reklamieren.	*Unfortunately we must complain about ...*
Wir müssen darauf hinweisen, daß ...	*We feel forced to point out that ...* ***or*** *We must draw your attention to the fact that ...*
Wir müssen darauf bestehen,daß ...	*We must insist that ...*
Wir erwarten Ihre Antwort.	*We look forward to your reply.*
Kiste Nr. ... enthält Artikel, die wir nicht bestellt haben.	*Crate no. ... contains items which we have not ordered.*

Beim Öffnen der Kiste stellten wir fest, daß ...	*On/Upon opening the crate we found that ...*
Wir können diese Waren nicht akzeptieren, da ...	*We cannot accept these goods as/ since ...*
Offensichtlich wurde ein Fehler gemacht.	*It is clear/obvious that an error/ mistake has been made.*
Wir müssen uns über die nachlässige Verpackung beschweren.	*We must complain about the unsatisfactory/careless manner of packing.*
Die Sendung kam in mangelhaftem Zustand an.	*The consignment arrived in a defective condition.*
Die Waren waren bei der Anlieferung schwer beschädigt.	*The goods were badly damaged when delivered.*
Wir hoffen, daß ein solcher Fehler nicht wieder vorkommt.	*We hope/trust that such an error will not occur/happen again.*
Beim Wiegen des Sackes stellten wir fest, daß ... Kilo am Gewicht fehlt.	*On/Upon weighing the bag we found that it was ... kilos underweight.*
Wir müssen Sie davon unterrichten, daß wir uns über Ihre sonst ausgezeichnete Waren beschweren müssen.	*We must notify/inform/advise you that we feel forced to complain about your otherwise/normally/usually excellent goods.*
Die jetzige Sendung ist keineswegs zufriedenstellend.	*The most recent consignment is totally/ highly/completely unsatisfactory/ unacceptable.*
Leider sind die Geräte für den beabsichtigten Zweck völlig ungeeignet.	*Unfortunately, the machines are totally unsuitable for the intended purpose.*
Die Qualität des gelieferten Artikels entspricht bei weitem nicht der des Musters.	*The quality of the item delivered fails to correspond to that of the sample whatsoever.*
Wenn diese Sendung nicht bis ... hier eintrifft, sehen wir uns genötigt, den Auftrag zu stornieren, da wir nicht länger auf die Geräte warten können.	*Should the consignment fail to arrive here by ..., we see ourselves forced to cancel the order since we cannot wait for the machines any longer.*

Bankangelegenheiten	
Bitte eröffnen Sie ein Konto.	*Please open an account.*
Bitte schließen Sie das Konto Nr. ...	*Please close account no. ...*
Wir wären dankbar, wenn sie uns einen Kredit von ... gewähren würden.	*We would be grateful if you would arrange a credit of ...*
Bitte, gewähren Sie uns ein Darlehen von ... für die Zeit von ...	*Please allow us a loan of ... for a period of ...*
Bitte, veranlassen Sie die Überweisung von ... am ersten dieses Monats.	*Please arrange the transfer the amount of ... on the first of this month.*
Bitte, überweisen Sie ... von unserem laufenden Konto bei Ihrer Geschäftsstelle auf das Konto der Firma ... bei Ihrer Zweigstelle in ...	*Please be kind enough to transfer ... from our account at your branch to the account of ... at your ... branch.*
Bitte sperren Sie die Zahlung des obigen Schecks. Bitte stellen Sie mit Wirkung vom ... die monatlichen Zahlung an ...	*Please stop payment of the above cheque.* *Please cease/discontiniue/cancel the monthly payments to ... with effect from ...*
Der Scheck ist anscheinend in der Post verlorengegangen.	*The cheque seems/appears to have been lost in he post.*

Bewerbungen	
Ich beziehe mich auf Ihre Anzeige in ... vom ...	*With reference to you advertisement in ... dated ...*
Ich bewerbe mich um den Posten eines ...	*I am applying for the post of a ...*
Ich möchte mich um die Stelle bewerben.	*I should/would like to apply for the post.*
Ich habe von ... gehört, daß in Ihrer Abteilung die Stelle eines Verkäufers frei ist.	*I understand from ... that there is an opening for a sales man in your department.* ***or** ...*

	has led me to understand that you are seeking to fill a vacancy for a sales man in your department
Augenblicklich bin ich als Buchhalter tätig.	*At the moment I am employed as an accountant.* ***or*** *At present I work as a book keeper.*
Augenblicklich bin ich arbeitslos.	*At the moment I am out of work.* *1) At present I am seeking employment.* *2) I am between jobs for the time being.* *3) I am, at the moment, looking for a position.*
Während der letzten vier Jahren ...	*During the last four years ...*
Eine Firma Ihrer Größe bietet mir bessere Möglichkeiten/Aussichten.	*A large company like yours offers better/improved opportunities/ prospects.*
Ich möchte meine jetzige Stelle aufgeben, weil ich hier nur beschränkte Möglichkeiten habe, verantwortungsvolle Tätigkeiten zu übernehmen.	*I wish to leave my present post as I see only limited opportunities of assuming more responibilities.* ***or*** *I would like to give up my current position since it presents very few possiblities for assuming greater responsibility.*
Ich besuchte ... die Schule/Universität ... Jahre lang.	I *attended ... school/university for ... years.*
1985 schloß ich meine Ausbildung an der Universität ab.	*I graduated in 1985.*
Vom ... bis ... habe ich bei der Firma ... in ... meine Ausbildung erhalten.	*From the year ... to the year ... I served an apprenticeship with ... in ...*
Ich habe gute Russischkenntnisse	*I have a good/fair knowledge of Russian*

Ich spreche fließend Arabisch und Französisch.	*I speak fluent Arabic and French.*
Ich wäre äußerst dankbar, wenn Sie mir ein Vorstellungsgespräch gewähren würden.	*I should/would be extremely grateful if I could have an interview* **or** *I would appreciate it very much if you granted me an interview.*
Ich wäre für die Möglichkeit eines Vorstellungsgesprächs dankbar.	*I would appreciate the opportunity of having an interview.*
Ich werde sehr gerne zu einem Vorstellungsgespräch kommen.	*I should be most pleased to attend an interview.*
Ich werde am ... verfügbar sein.	*I shall be available on ...*
Ich sehe dem Erhalt einer positiven Antwort gerne entgegen.	*I look forward to receiving a positive/ favourable reply.*

Termine und Einladungen

Am Dienstag, dem ... werde ich wieder in ... sein.	*I shall/will be again be in ... on Tuesday ...*
Bitte schlagen Sie einen anderen Tag/ eine andere Zeit vor, falls diese Zeit/ dieser Tag Ihnen nicht paßt.	*Please suggest an alternative day/ time if this time/date does not suit you.*
Bitte, rufen Sie mich an.	*Please give me a ring.*
Eine Nachricht wird mich im Büro erreichen.	*A message will reach me in the office.*
Ich freue mich darauf, Sie wieder zu sehen.	*It will be a pleasure to see you again.*
Ich freue mich sehr, Sie zu treffen.	*I will be delighted to meet you.*
Ich freue mich, Sie zu treffen.	*I look forward to meeting you.*
Ich würde die Gelegenheit begrüßen, das Problem mit Ihnen persönlich zu besprechen.	*I would/should welcome the chance/ opportunity of discussing the problem with you personally.*

Ich würde die Gelegenheit, Sie zu treffen, schätzen, um Einzelheiten zu besprechen.	*I would appreciate the chance/opportunity of meeting/seeing/getting together with you in order to discuss details.*
Ich würde mich freuen, wenn Sie eine Zeit und ein Datum vorschlagen würden, um ...	*I would be pleased/happy/glad if you would suggest a time and date to ...*
Ich würde Sie gerne aufsuchen ...	*I would like to call on you ...*
Vielleicht könnten Sie sich mit mir so bald wie möglich in Verbindung setzen.	*Perhaps it would be possible for you to get in touch with me as soon as you can.* **or** *Maybe you could contact me as soon as possible.*
Wäre es überhaupt möglich, einen anderen Termin zu vereinbaren?	*Would it be at all possible to arrange another meeting?*
Wenn Sie mich anrufen, wäre es vielleicht möglich, einen Termin irgendwann im nächsten Monat zu vereinbaren.	*If you rang me up/gave me a ring it would be perhaps possible to sort out/fix/arrange a meeting sometime next month.*
Würde Ihnen ... um ... passen?	*Would ... on ... suit you?* **or** *Would ... on ... be convenient?*
Ein Termin am Nachmittag würde mir besser passen.	*An afternoon appointment/meeting would suit me best.*
Ich werde die ganze Woche im ... Hotel sein, und eine Nachricht wird mich hier sicher erreichen.	*I shall be spending the whole week at the ... Hotel where a message will certainly reach me.*
Leider muß ich das vereinbarte Zusammentreffen für den ... verschieben.	*Unfortunately I will have to postpone/put off the appointment made for ...*
Leider müssen wir das Zusammentreffen am nächsten ... absagen.	*We are sorry but we must cancel the meeting planned for next ...*

Herr ... bedauert sehr, daß er nicht in seinem Büro war, als Ihr Vertreter gestern vorbeikam.	*Mr ... regrets it very much but he was not in the office when your representative called.*
Er wurde unerwartet zu der Fabrik in ... gerufen.	*He was unexpectedly called over to the plant in ...*
Vielen Dank für Ihre freundliche Einladung.	*Thank you very much for your kind invitation.*
Es hat mich äußerst gefreut, Ihrem Brief vom ... zu entnehmen, daß Sie und Ihr Mann in März in ... sein werden.	*I was most pleased to learn from your letter dated ... that you and your husband will be in ... in March.*

Niederlassungen planen

Wenn Sie Ihre Firma hierher verlegen, bieten sich mehrere Vorteile.	*Moving your company here will result in several advantages.*
Es gibt gute Straßen und Bahnverbindungen.	*There are good road and rail connections.*
Die Regierung wird Anreize bieten.	*The government will offer incentives.*
Grundstücke können gepachtet werden.	*Sites are available for rent.*
Sie können die Grundstücke besichtigen	*You can inspect the sites*
Es gibt Fabriken, die zu sofortiger Nutzung zur Verfügung stehen.	*There are factories available for immediate use.*
Falls Sie Ihre Fabrik erweitern möchten, wird es kein Problem geben, da angrenzendes Bauland verfügbar ist.	*If you wish to expand your factory there will be no problem as there is building land ajoining.*
Sonderfinanzierungen werden gewährt.	*Special loans are available.*

Vocabulary

A

ability	Fähigkeit
able; be ~ to do	etwas können
abroad	im Ausland
accept	annehmen
accept a draft	eine Tratte mit einem Akzept versehen
acceptance	Annahme
accommodation	Unterkunft
accompany	begleiten
accordance; in ~ with	gemäß, entsprechend
according to	entsprechend
accordingly	dementsprechend
account	Rechnung, Konto
accountant	Buchhalter
accounts department	Buchhaltungsabteilung
accustomed to	gewöhnt daran
acknowledgement	Bestätigung, Auftragsbestätigung
act as an agent	als Agent arbeiten
actually	eigentlich, in der Tat
addition; in ~	außerdem
admit	zugeben
advance; in ~	im voraus
advantage	Vorteil
advertise	annoncieren, Werbung machen
advertisement	Annonce, Anzeige
advise	verständigen, unterrichten, beraten
agency	Agentur
agency agreement	Vertretervertrag
agent	Vertreter
agreed	vereinbart
agreed; as ~	wie vereinbart
agreed condition	vereinbarte Bedingung
allow	gewähren
although	obwohl
amount	Betrag
annul	annullieren
anyway	trotzdem
apart from	abgesehen von
apologise	sich entschuldigen
applicant	Bewerber

application	Bewerbung
apply for	bewerben um
apply on spec	sich auf gut Glück bewerben
appoint	ernennen
appreciate	zu schätzen wissen, gerne zur Kenntnis nehmen
appreciative	dankbar
area	Gebiet
arrival	Ankunft
arrive	ankommen
as a result of	als Folge
as far as … is concerned	was … betrifft
as soon as	so bald wie
as well as	sowie
assistance	Hilfe
assume	annehmen
assure	versichern
assure; ~ somebody of something	jemanden etwas versichern
at all	überhaupt
at least	mindestens
at the latest	spätestens
attach	beiheften
attached	beigeheftet, beiliegend
attention (draw attention to something.)	Aufmerksamkeit (auf etwas lenken)
attention; for the ~ of…	zu Händen von …
attention; your order will receive ~	Ihre Bestellung wird bearbeitet
attention; it has come to our ~	wir sind darauf aufmerksam geworden
availability	Vorrätigkeit
available	vorrätig, lieferbar
avoid	vermeiden

B

badly bruised (fruit)	(Obst) mit schlimmen Druckstellen
balance	Kontostand, Saldo, begleichen
balance sheet	Bilanz
banking	Bankwesen
basic	einfach
believe	glauben
bend	Bogen

bet	wetten
beyond our control	nicht in unserer Hand liegend
bill	Rechnung
bill of exchange	übertragbare Zahlungsanweisung, Wechsel
bill of lading	Seefrachtbrief / Konnossement
biscuit	Keks
board of directors	Vorstand
booth	Stand
boring	langweilig
box	Karton
bracket	Anschluß
branch	Filiale
breach of contract	Vertragsbruch
brochure	Prospekt
builder	Bauunternehmer
bulk order	Großauftrag
business practice	Geschäftspraxis
business relationship	Geschäftsbeziehung
buyer	Käufer, Einkäufer
by the same post	mit gleicher Post

C

caller	Anrufer
cancel	stornieren
cancellation	Stornierung
candidature	Kandidatur
cargo	Fracht
carry out	ausführen
case	Kiste, Fall
cash discount	Skonto
catalogue	Katalog
cause	verursachen/Ursache
cautious	vorsichtig
certain	bestimmt
certainly not	sicher nicht
certificate	Zeugnis
Chamber of Industry and Commerce	Industrie- und Handelskammer
chap	Kerl
charge; in ~	verantwortlich

charity	Wohltätigkeitsverein
charming	charmant
chat me up	mich anquatschen
cheap	billig
chief	Haupt-
CIF (Cost, Insurance, Freight)	Kosten, Versicherung, Fracht
circumstance	Umstand
clear	begleichen
clear a bill	eine Rechnung begleichen
clearly	offensichtlich
clerk	Büroangestellte
close to	in der Nähe von
clothing	Kleidung
coal	Kohle
collect payment	einziehen, Inkasso durchführen
come up to	entsprechen
common	gemeinsam
comparison	Vergleich
compel	zwingen
competition	Konkurrenz
competitive	konkurrenzfähig
complain	beklagen, Beschwerde einlegen
complaint	Beschwerde
complete	ausführen
complete a form	ein Formular ausfüllen
concern	Sorge, Besorgnis
concerning	bezüglich, hinsichtlich
condition	Bedingung
condition of payment	Zahlungsbedingung
confidence	Vertrauen
confidential	vertraulich
confirm	bestätigen
consequence	Folge
consequence; as a ~	als Folge
consider	denken, betrachten, glauben
considerable	groß, erheblich, beträchtlich
considerable; with ~ regret	mit großem Bedauern
consideration; take into ~	in Betracht ziehen
consignment	Lieferung, Sendung
contact	sich in Verbindung setzen
contain	enthalten

Continent	Kontinentaleuropa
contract	Vertrag
contribute	beitragen
convenient time	passende Zeit
convinced; to be ~	sicher sein, überzeugt sein
copper pipe	Kupferrohr
corner shop	Laden an der Ecke
correspond	entsprechen
council	Verwaltung
counter-offer	Gegenangebot
couple of	ein paar
courtesy	Höflichkeit
cover for	einspringen für
covering letter	Begleitbrief
crate	Kiste
credit enquiry agency	Kreditauskunftei
credit facility	Kreditrahmen
creditworthiness	Kreditwürdigkeit
curious	neugierige
current	aktuell
current account	laufendes Konto
curriculum vitae (CV)	Lebenslauf
custom	Kundschaft
customer	Kunde
customs	Zoll
cut the costs	die Kosten reduzieren

D

dad	Papa
damaged	beschädigt
darling	Schatz, Liebling
dated	datiert
dates... to...	vom ... bis zum ...
day off	Tag frei
deadline	letzter Termin
deal with	fertig werden mit
debts	Schulden
decide	entscheiden; sich ~
defective	fehlerhaft, defekt
delay	Verspätung, Verzögerung

delighted	entzückt
delivery	Lieferung
delivery date	Liefertermin
delivery time	Lieferfrist
demand	Nachfrage
department	Abteilung
departure	Abreise
depending on	abhängig von
depending on	hier: je nachdem
deposit	deponieren, Einlage, Guthaben
despatch	senden, versenden
despatch advice	Versandanzeige
despite the fact that	trotz der Tatsache, daß
develop	entwickeln
develop a market	einen Markt erschließen
direct debit	Einzugsermächtigung
disappointed	enttäuscht
discount	Rabatt
display (on display)	Ausstellung (ausgestellt sein)
disposal; placed at the ~	zur Verfügung gestellt
disposal; at my disposal ~	zu meiner Verfügung
disregard	ignorieren, nicht beachten
distribute	verteilen
distribution	Verteilung
distributor	Verteiler, Großhändler
diving equipment	Tauchgeräte
do business	Geschäfte machen
domestic market	Binnenmarkt
don't worry	keine Sorge
draft	Tratte, gezogener Wechsel
dreadful	schrecklich
dried dates	getrocknete Datteln
drive me round the bend	mich verrückt machen
due	fällig
due to	infolge, wegen
due to	aufgrund, wegen
due; the goods are ~ to arrive on the ...	die Waren sollen eintreffen am ...
duration	Dauer
duty	Pflicht

E

early order discount	Frühdispositionsrabatt
education	Ausbildung
effect	ausführen
elsewhere	anderswo
embassy	Botschaft
employed	beschäftigt sein
employee	Arbeitnehmer
enclose	beilegen
enclosed	beiliegend
enquire	fragen, erkundigen
enquirer	Fragesteller
enquiry	Anfrage
enterprising	unternehmungslustig
entirely	völlig
equipment	Geräte, Ausrüstung
error	Fehler
especially	besonders
essential	sehr wichtig
establish	gründen, bilden
estimate	schätzen
evaluate	einschätzen, beurteilen
excess; in ~ of	übersteigend, mehr als
excuse	Ausrede
execute	ausführen
execute orders	Bestellungen ausführen
execution	Ausführung
exhibition	Ausstellung
expanding	expandierend
expectations	Erwartungen
expensive	teuer
experience	Erfahrung
experienced	erfahren
explain	erklären
explanation	Erklärung
extension	Verlängerung
extremely	äußerst

F

facility	Einrichtung, Möglichkeit
facility	Einrichtung
factory	Fabrik
fail to do	etwas nicht tun, etwas unterlassen
failure	Mißerfolg, Scheitern
faith; in good ~	in gutem Glauben
familiar	vertraut
favour; in your favour ~	zu Ihren Gunsten
filing cabinet	Aktenschrank
fill in	ausfüllen
final demand	letzte Mahnung
finalize	endgültig festlegen
finally	endlich
firm	bestimmt, fest, streng
fix up	arrangieren
following	folgende
food	Lebensmittel
force	zwingen
force; ~ somebody to do something	jemanden zwingen, etwas zu tun
foreign language	Fremdsprache
foreign trade	Außenhandel
form	Formular
forward	befördern, senden
forwarding agent	Spediteur
freight rate	Frachtsatz
frozen	blockiert
fulfil	erfüllen
furnish with something	mit etwas versorgen
further	weiter
future	Zukunft

G

GCE A Level	Abi
GCE O Level	mittlere Reife
general public	Publikum, Öffentlichkeit
generate (be generated)	entstehen
gat about	viel herumkommen

get a name	bekannt werden
get in touch with	sich in Verbindung setzen
glad	froh
go slow	Bummelstreik
going on (what is going on)	was los ist
good grief!	mein Gott!
good mood	gute Laune
good time; in ~	rechtzeitig
good will	Wohlwollen
goods	Waren
grant	gewähren
grant an agency	eine Vertretung übertragen
grateful	dankbar

H

hairy	haarig
handle	bearbeiten
hangover	Kater
have a go at something	versuchen, etwas zu tun
have trouble	Probleme haben
head	Leiter
head of sales	Leiter der Verkaufsabteilung
heating engineering	Heizungsinstallateur
heating equipment	Heizgerät
hesitate	zögern
hire	einstellen
hold on!	Moment mal!
hold the view that	der Ansicht sein
hold up	verspäten/Verspätung
hopefully	hoffentlich
hopeless	hoffnungslos
however	jedoch

I

I'd better	ich sollte, es wäre besser
ice skating	Eislauf
illustrated literature	Bildmaterial
immediate	sofortig
importance	Wichtigkeit

impression	Eindruck
in general	im allgemeinen
in the black	in den schwarzen Zahlen
in the press	in der Presse
in the red	in den roten Zahlen
in this case	in diesem Fall
in writing	schriftlich
in your favour	zu Ihren Gunsten
inability	Unfähigkeit
incentive	Anreiz
include	einschließen
including	einschließlich
inconvenience	Unbequemlichkeit, Unannehmlichkeit
incredidible	unglaublich
indicate	deuten auf
industrial action	Arbeitskampfmaßnahmen
influence	beeinflussen
inspect	besichtigen
inspection	Kontrolle
instead of	anstelle
instruct	anweisen
instruction/instruct	Anweisung, anweisen
insurance	Versicherung
insurance certificate	Versicherungszertifikat
insurance policy	Versicherungspolice
intend	beabsichtigen
interest (rate of interest)	Zinsen (Zinssatz)
interview	Vorstellungsgespräch
investigate	überprüfen
invitation/invite	Einladung, einladen
invoice	Warenrechnung
involved	beteiligt
issue a letter of credit	ein Akkreditiv ausstellen
item	Artikel

J

joint owner	Mitbesitzer
junior	Bürogehilfe

K

keep up with	Schritt halten mit
kindly	freundlicherweise

L

law	Gesetz
law; go to ~	vors Gericht gehen
lazy	faul
lead to	dazu führen
leading	führend, wichtig
legal action	Klage
legal proceedings	Verfahren, Gerichtsverhandlung
legally binding	verbindlich
lending department	Kreditabteilung
let down	enttäuschen
let somebody have something	jemandem etwas schicken
let us have	schicken Sie uns
letter of credit	Akkreditiv, Kreditbrief
level	Ebene
libel	Verleumdung
limited	beschränkt
line	Branche
lined with styrofoam	mit Schaumstoff ausgekleidet
list	auflisten
loan	Darlehen
local government	Kommunalverwaltung
local market	örtlicher Markt
locate something	etwas finden
location	Lage, Örtlichkeit
look for	suchen nach
look forward to	sich freuen auf
look into	prüfen
loss	Verlust
lost	verloren
luckily	zum Glück

M

make it (can you make it?)	schaffen (schaffen Sie es?)
make up	Zusammensetzung
mark	beschriften
market a product	etwas auf den Markt bringen
matter	Sache, Angelegenheit
meet; ~ a date	einen Termin einhalten
meet up	treffen
member	Mitglied
mention	erwähnen
message	Nachricht
ministry	Ministerium
misunderstanding	Mißverständnis
monk	Mönch

N

need	Bedürfnis
neighbouring	angrenzend, benachbart
note	zur Kenntnis nehmen
number	numerieren

O

obtain	bekommen, erhalten
occasion	Gelegenheit, Anlaß
occur	vorkommen, passieren
offer	Angebot
offer	anbieten
old-fashioned	altmodisch
on my arrival	bei meiner Ankunft
on receipt	nach Eingang
on time	pünktlich
opinion; be of the ~	der Meinung sein
opportunity	Möglichkeit
order	Auftrag
order book	Auftragsbuch
order form	Bestell-Formular
outstanding	ausstehend
overdraft	Überziehung

overdraw	überziehen
overdue	überfällig
overlook	übersehen
overripe	überreif
overseas	Übersee
overseas market	Überseemarkt
oversight	Versehen
overtime	Überstunden
owing to	infolge
owner	Besitzer

P

participate	teilnehmen
participation	Teilnahme
pass	vergehen
past	vergangen
pay up	zurückzahlen
payable	zahlbar
payment	Zahlung
perform	leisten, durchführen
performance	Leistung
perishable	leicht verderblich
pick up	abholen
pipe	Rohr
place an order	einen Auftrag erteilen
plant	Anlage, Fabrik
pleased to	sich freuen
point out	hinweisen auf, betonen
polite	höflich
pompous	schwülstig
port of call	Anlaufhafen
post	Stelle
postage	Porto
practice	Gewohnheit, Verfahrensweise
precise	genau
prepared	bereit
previous	vorherig, vorhergehend, früher
price list	Preisliste
pride	Stolz
prior to	vor, bevor

priority	Vorrang
probably	wahrscheinlich
promise	Versprechen
promote	fördern
proposal	Vorschlag
prospect	Aussicht
prove	beweisen
provide	liefern
provide with	mit etwas versorgen
pull somebody's leg	jemanden auf den Arm nehmen
punctuation	Zeichensetzung
purchasing department	Einkaufsabteilung
put forward	vorschlagen
put in touch/contact	sich in Verbindung setzen

Q

quantity discount	Mengenrabatt
query	Frage
quid (slang for pound)	Eier (Dialekt für Geld)
quota	Kontingent
quotation	Kostenvoranschlag, Preisangabe

R

raise	Gehaltserhöhung
range	Sortiment, Auswahl
rate	Satz, Kurs
ready market; find a ~	einen guten Markt finden
reason	Vernunft, Grund
receipt; in ~	im Besitz
receive	erhalten
recent	neulich
reception	Empfang
refer to	sich beziehen auf
reference	Referenz, Zeugnis
refund	zurückzahlen
regarding	in bezug auf
regret	bedauern
regrettably	bedauerlicherweise
regular	regelmäßig

regular order	regelmäßiger Auftrag
relation	Beziehung
relationship	Beziehung
relative	Verwandte
reliable	zuverlässig
remark	Bemerkung
remind somebody of	erinnern; jemanden ~ an
remittance	Zahlung
rent	mieten
replacement	Ersatz
reply	antworten/Antwort
report	Bericht, berichten
representative	Vertreter
reputable	seriös, solide
request	bitten, ersuchen, Bitte
require	benötigen, erfordern
requirement	Bedarf, Bedürfnis
respected	angesehen
response	Antwort
result in	führen zu
retailer	Einzelhändler
right	Recht
right	richtig
rise	Erhöhung (Geld)
risky	riskant

S

sail	abfahren, auslaufen
sales condition	Verkaufsbedingung
sales department	Verkaufsabteilung
sample	Muster
satisfy	zufriedenstellen
saturated	gesättigt
savings account	Sparkonto
security	Sicherheit
seller	Verkäufer
service	Dienstleistung
set up	gründen, einrichten
settle	erledigen, klären
settle a bill	begleichen

settlement	Bezahlung
ship	versenden, verschiffen
shipment	Sendung, Verschiffung
shipowner	Reederei
shipping agent	Reedereivertreter
shipping documents	Versanddokumente
shipping instructions	Versandanweisungen
shop steward	Arbeitnehmervertreter
shorthand	Kurzschrift
shortly	bald
sight draft	Sichtwechsel
site	Gelände, Stelle, Grundstück
situations vacant	Stellenangebote
size	Größe
slander	Beleidigung
slightly	etwas, ein kleines bißchen
slip of paper	Blatt Papier
smart	schick
solicit	verlangen
solicitor	Anwalt
solvency	Zahlungsfähigkeit
sort out	erledigen
space	Platz, Raum
spare no effort	keine Mühe scheuen
special delivery	Sonderlieferung
spelling	Rechtschreibung
spelling mistake	Rechtschreibfehler
spoilt	verdorben
spot	Stelle
square	Viereck
stand	Stand
stand in	einspringen, vertreten
standing	Ruf
standing; of many years' ~	mit einem langjährigen guten Ruf
standing order	Dauerauftrag
stay	Aufenthalt
stay competitive	konkurrenzfähig bleiben
stock; from ~	ab Lager
stock; in ~	auf Lager
store	Lager
stress	betonen

strictest	strengstens
strictly	streng
subject to change without notice	Preisänderung vorbehalten
submit	einreichen, unterbreiten
subsidiary	Tochtergesellschaft
substantial	wesentlich
success	Erfolg
successful	erfolgreich
sufficient	ausreichend
suggest	vorschlagen
suggestion	Vorschlag
suitable	geeignet
supplier	Lieferant
supply	beliefern
suppose	annehmen, vermuten
surprise	überraschen
surprised	überrascht
suspend an account	ein Konto sperren

T

T-joint	T-Stück
take action	etwas unternehmen, Schritte unternehmen
take part	teilnehmen
tariff	Zoll
temporary	vorübergehend
term	Bedingung
terminate	lösen
terms of payment	Zahlungsbedingungen
think up	erfinden, ausdenken
thorough	gründlich
threaten	drohen
timber	Holz, Bauholz
tin of baked beans	Dose
to call attention to	auf etwas aufmerksam machen
tools	Werkzeuge
to our satisfaction	zu unserer Zufriedenheit
trade	Handel, Geschäft
trade discount	Händlerrabatt
trade fair	Handelsmesse

trade references	Handelsreferenz
trainee	Auszubildender
transaction	Geschäft, Transaktion, Abwicklung
transfer	überweisen, Überweisung
transport cost	Transportkosten
treat	behandeln
triplet	Drilling
tropical disease	tropische Krankheit
truck	Lastwagen
trusted	vertrauenswürdig

U

unable	unfähig
underweight	untergewichtig
union	Gewerkschaft
unit	Einheit
unless	es sei denn, wenn nicht
unreliable	unzuverlässig
unsatisfactory	nicht zufriedenstellend
unsolicited	unverlangt, nicht bestellt
untidy	unordentlich
upon; ~ opening	bei (beim Öffnen)
urgently	dringend
useful	nützlich

V

vacancy	freie Stelle
valid	gültig
valid until	gültig bis
valuable	wertvoll
variety	Vielfalt, Auswahl
various	verschieden
virtually	nahezu, fast
vital	lebenswichtig
vitals	lebenswichtige Organe
voluntary work	freiwillige Arbeit
vouch for	sich verbürgen für

W

wage	Lohn
waste	verschwenden
water pumps	Wasserpumpe
weed out	aussieben
weigh	wiegen
well established	gut eingeführt
what on earth!	was in aller Welt!
what's more	außerdem
whatever	wie auch immer
wholesale	Großhandel
wholesaler	Großhändler
wide range	große Auswahl
willing to	bereit zu
with a view to	mit der Absicht, etwas zu tun
with regard to	hinsichtlich, in bezug auf
withdraw	abheben
withdraw an offer	ein Angebot zurückziehen
without engagement	ohne Verpflichtung
word gets round that ...	man munkelt, daß ...
work to rule	Dienst nach Vorschrift
wrong (what's wrong?)	falsch *(*was ist los?)